S0-BFC-669

Volume Five:

King Vidor
John Cromwell
Mervyn LeRoy

by
Clive Denton
Kingsley Canham

This series spotlights the work of the many professional directors at work in Hollywood during its heyday—talents who might otherwise be ignored by film students and historians. This volume contains monographs on, and very detailed filmographies of King Vidor, John Cromwell, and Mervyn LeRoy, who between them made scores of familiar movies with a competence and a gloss now rarely seen in the cinema.

$4.95

In the same series,
produced by THE TANTIVY PRESS
and edited by Peter Cowie:

THE MARX BROTHERS Their World of Comedy by Allen Eyles
HORROR IN THE CINEMA by Ivan Butler
HOLLYWOOD IN THE TWENTIES by David Robinson
HOLLYWOOD IN THE THIRTIES by John Baxter
HOLLYWOOD IN THE FORTIES by Charles Higham and Joel Greenberg
HOLLYWOOD IN THE FIFTIES by Gordon Gow
HOLLYWOOD IN THE SIXTIES by John Baxter
HOLLYWOOD TODAY by Allen Eyles and Pat Billings
RELIGION IN THE CINEMA by Ivan Butler
THE CINEMA OF FRITZ LANG by Paul M. Jensen
THE CINEMA OF JOHN FRANKENHEIMER by Gerald Pratley
SCIENCE FICTION IN THE CINEMA by John Baxter
THE CINEMA OF FRANCOIS TRUFFAUT by Graham Petrie
THE CINEMA OF ROMAN POLANSKI by Ivan Butler
THE CINEMA OF JOSEF VON STERNBERG by John Baxter
EARLY AMERICAN CINEMA by Anthony Slide
GRIFFITH & THE RISE OF HOLLYWOOD by Paul O'Dell
THE CINEMA OF CARL DREYER by Tom Milne
THE CINEMA OF JOHN FORD by John Baxter
THE CINEMA OF OTTO PREMINGER by Gerald Pratley
THE CINEMA OF ANDRZEJ WAJDA by Boleslaw Michalek
THE ANIMATED FILM by Ralph Stephenson
THE HOLLYWOOD PROFESSIONALS
    (Vol. 1: Curtiz, Walsh, Hathaway)
    (Vol. 2: King, Wood, Milestone)
    (Vol. 3: Hawks, Borzage, Ulmer)
    (Vol. 4: Browning, Siegel)

The Hollywood Professionals

KING VIDOR

by Clive Denton

JOHN CROMWELL

by Kingsley Canham

MERVYN LeROY

by Kingsley Canham

THE TANTIVY PRESS, LONDON
A. S. BARNES & CO., NEW YORK

Cover design by Stefan Dreja

First Published 1976
Copyright © 1976 by The Tantivy Press.
Library of Congress Catalogue Card No. 72-1786
SBN 0-904208-11-7 (U.K.)
ISBN 0-498-01689-7 (U.S.A.)

Printed in the United States of America

Contents

King Vidor: a Texas Poet

King Vidor is a poet, of man and nature. Although the concept of "poetry in the cinema" has been badly over-used, I beg leave to raise it once more. He is a rarity—a Texas poet. Where Henry King's films reflect the mellowness of his native Virginia, Vidor brings the breadth of a Texas vision. Breadth but not, fortunately, brashness. It is strange but perhaps fitting that his most usual American setting is not Texas but the mid-West. There is no denying Vidor's poetic approach both to open spaces and interior emotions—visually to sunsets, swamps and dusty city streets, thematically to love, death, elation, fear, survival. True poetry, of course, must have a heart and a meaning, otherwise it is mere decoration. Vidor has consistently shown great concern for people and their problems—by insisting that Metro make *The Crowd* and make it truthfully, by sinking his own resources into *Our Daily Bread*. There is compassion and understanding, at least in the margin, of even those least promising assignments with which, like almost all directors, he has sometimes marked time in order to stay in the race. His humanity is evident. Anybody who meets him for five minutes can experience his kindliness and cordiality. Yet I would think it misleading to describe his films as, primarily, *humanistic*. I would so describe the work of Henry King but Vidor is far more an *epic* poet, given to large, almost abstract expressions of man's role in nature and society. His characters—suffering or succeeding, always striving in any case—have to carry symbolic weight to an extent rare in American cinema. His hero is frequently an "Everyman"—John Gilbert in *The Big Parade* (whose character name is actually Apperson), James Murray in *The Crowd*. Vidor's own word for this honourable human average is more folksy. He calls him "Mr. Anyman."

King Vidor with testimonial on completion of STELLA DALLAS

If King Vidor is a poet, he is a poet compelled far too often to work in prose. Hollywood rarely allows true poetic feeling to flow for more than, at most, a reel at a time. Where the intention is epic, the result may be merely "Epic", something alas quite different. Where the verse should be meaningfully simple, the style is all too often mundane. Hollywood's chief bogeyman is that old bore, the plot. Vidor has been badly hemmed in by indifferent, yet time-consuming, stories. It is hard to say how much this is his fault and how much his misfortune. I wish that he could have continued his career into the Sixties, when plots as such became less constricting and such previously taboo approaches as symbolism and expressionism began to have a certain amount of play. As it is, there is almost as much to regret as to applaud in his work between the two masterpieces, widely separated in time, *The Crowd* and *War and Peace*. Andrew Sarris made a characteristically perceptive statement (though I find it a little too harsh): "he has created more great moments and fewer great films than any director of his rank." Greatness there is in Vidor, however we may argue the ebb and flow of his talent and opportunities. For greatness we should always be grateful.

EARLY DAYS

When this century was still in its teens, a suburb of Los Angeles, California, was already pulling itself up by rough boot strings in preparation for great years to come. Hollywood, though still rough-and-ready, was proving a magnet drawing the talents of ambitious young men who would become crucial to its later prosperity. An actor, a writer, a stuntman or extra or jack-of-all-trades could learn the new rules of films by working in them, could add a few rules of his own and in a very short time could emerge as John Ford or Raoul Walsh or Allan Dwan. These men's entry into Hollywood is now a matter of history but, naturally, nobody knew it at the time. They arrived from all over the country, on different and mostly forgotten dates, carried by unrecorded trains and buses and cars. King Vidor made the journey from Texas, by car and steamer, in 1915. He had what most of his colleagues did not have: a little experience. Unusually, he had begun film-making at home.

As a boy in Galveston, Vidor was pursuing a formal education but his seduction away from it began when he took a summer job at the local nickelodeon. He was ticket taker and relief projectionist—the "relief" including his thankfulness that the nitrate film did not, as he feared, burst into flames the first time he threw the projection switch. As he describes his youthful feelings, what would become a passion for the art of film began more as a matter of scientific curiosity. He wanted to know how movies could be made—made at all, that is, let alone made well.

In 1913, with a friend and a home-made camera, Vidor took some shots of a cyclone which was whirling around Galveston. Because of the local interest in this storm, the pictures were bought and shown quite widely in the state. Vidor's career had begun, but in the next two years it kept threatening to end as the young man in Texas tried to inch into an industry already controlled from New York—and Hollywood. So, after more local filming including documentary footage sold as contributions to the early newsreels, King and his young bride Florence Vidor began an arduous trip to Hollywood. The year was 1915. With hope, energy and a pressing lack of money, taking footage for future sale along the way, they travelled their own personal Yellow Brick Road.

Florence Vidor had dreamed of being a movie actress while she was still Florence Arto* back in Galveston. The attentions of

---

* She was born as Florence Cobb, later assuming the surname Arto when her mother re-married.

a young, self-styled film director right at home soon won her matrimonially and her own ambitions and sharing of his dreams must have helped her husband's enthusiasm greatly. She became his usual leading lady on screen also, first in Texas and then in Hollywood until 1922. Her later directors included, notably, Ernst Lubitsch (*The Marriage Circle* [1924], *The Patriot* [1928]). With growing success attending both husband and wife, it is ironic that in the future divorce would ensue. (King Vidor was later married to actress Eleanor Boardman and then, most lastingly, to Elizabeth Hill, who had been his script girl and who collaborated on many of his films' screenplays including *Our Daily Bread*).

At first, the Vidors had to struggle for survival in Hollywood. They found various kinds of movie employment—and unemployment. King was an extra and a writer while living round the corner from the great Babylon set erected by D. W. Griffith for *Intolerance.* He was able to watch Griffith directing and says he learned an enormous amount from this experience. His own opportunities came from sources outside the big studios. A series of short films about juvenile crime and rehabilitation was financed by Judge Willis Brown. The judge played himself in each miniature drama, under young Vidor's direction. Then at last came the chance to make a feature. *The Turn of the Road,* improbably produced by a group of medical men, was designed to promote and illustrate beliefs of Christian Scientists. It was a notable commercial success and led to offers from the big studios. Vidor was soon able to open his own small movie lot. Picturesquely named Vidor Village, it housed the production of *The Jack-knife Man, The Family Honor* and *The Sky Pilot.* These films, released by First National, did not return their costs quickly enough for Vidor Village to survive and so the director found himself at Metro, directing Laurette Taylor in a film of her stage success, *Peg o' My Heart.* As Metro moved towards being Metro-Goldwyn-Mayer, Vidor began his long association with the lion's studio (or should that be the lion's den?).

WAR, WHEAT AND STEEL

One day at M-G-M in 1925, King Vidor and Irving Thalberg were discussing movies. Vidor, after ten years in Hollywood, wanted to make a bigger film, a better film, a more meaningful film than anything he had done so far. Thalberg gave him a choice of subjects—or at least a *chance* of a choice, if he should like any of Vidor's ideas. The reply, apparently given almost intuitively and without long thought, was to resound throughout the director's work for years ahead. Vidor offered to make Thalberg a film on one of three subjects: war, wheat and steel. The always shrewd M-G-M production head chose war, resulting in *The Big Parade*. Later in his career Vidor would come to wheat (in *Our Daily Bread*, 1934) and steel (*An American Romance*, 1944). But Thalberg responded to war as a subject, probably on the grounds that a strong personal story is more implicit in warfare than in a corn field or a factory. The enormous popular success of *The Big Parade* reflects the film's canny balance of an overwhelming social subject with an intimate, personal tale, the experiences of an average American soldier (John Gilbert) in combat.

The Big Parade brought Vidor immense prestige, within the film colony as well as outside, just as surely as *The Iron Horse* had ensured the rising fortunes of John Ford one year before. It is said to have grossed over fifteen million dollars on first release and was reissued, with music and effects, in 1931. So many war films have been made in the ensuing almost half-century that a little historical perspective is required to understand *The Big Parade*'s contemporary driving force and related public approval. The First World War had been shown rather sparingly since its

Tom O'Brien, John Gilbert and Karl Dane in THE BIG PARADE

close. It had been the war to end wars and the Twenties acted like it had succeeded in that happy objective. If war scenes *were* shown, they were chiefly background for a romance or an adventure. Not since Griffith's *Hearts of the World,* back in 1918, had war played a major role, been a symbolic character, as the scourge now became in *The Big Parade.* Added to this, the realistic and objective view of the mechanics and routines of fighting and marching and dying came across under Vidor's direction with great freshness and force. Some scenes are now legendary: the French girl running after the truck which is taking away the soldier she loves; the shell hole sequence between Gilbert and the young German he has mortally wounded; the very moving home-

Renee Adoree clutches John Gilbert in THE BIG PARADE

coming of the wounded Gilbert to his mother. Even so, *The Big Parade* today seems rather cool and uncommitted. The film, like its hero, experiences war, looks around at it, is wounded but survives. All this is neither tub-thumping nor pacifistic. Vidor's film has pain in it—otherwise it would be shallow indeed—but the pain is much less than cataclysmic, as it will be five years later in Milestone's *All Quiet on the Western Front*.

If we consider *The Big Parade*, *Our Daily Bread* and *An American Romance* as Vidor's trilogy on war, wheat and steel, then some qualification must be made about *Our Daily Bread*. Not being an M-G-M picture like the other two, it is made on a smaller scale. Nor does it fully represent the theme of "wheat".

Its main subject is the American Depression of the Thirties, but in the story the co-operative workers who band together on a farm do grow wheat and the saving of a precious crop by emergency irrigation provides the film's famous climax with a sense of excitement at the workings of nature rare in the cinema. Many years later, after the introduction of Cinerama, Vidor thought of making a film in that process called *The Land*. This would have done wheat proud—yards and yards of it on the wide screen. But nothing came of the idea, so we should be glad that at least *Our Daily Bread,* besides being a genuinely fine and honest achievement, does carry the wheat *motif* into film history.

Although *Our Daily Bread* is not an M-G-M film, it might well have been. Vidor was working mostly for that studio throughout the Thirties with occasional side trips to Goldwyn and elsewhere. He broached the subject to Thalberg but this time the producer was not responsive. Too much of a risk. Vidor tried other studios with equally negative results. Finally, he managed to raise money independently and to make the film on his own for United Artists release. As an early example of "free cinema," its faults and virtues have a special fascination. (Vidor has disarmingly confessed to one fault. The bad girl who tempts the married hero was put in for box-office insurance. She does rather jar in a film whose thematic villain is apathy, not adultery.)

It is hard to judge *An American Romance* because, more than any other Vidor film, it is obviously less impressive than it should have been. The lead figure of a poor immigrant who becomes rich and prosperous as America also grows and changes was intended to be played by Spencer Tracy. Vidor now bitterly regrets not changing his schedule to get Tracy but accepting instead Brian Donlevy who, although a serviceable actor, entirely lacks the charisma necessary for such a pivotal and, indeed, symbolic role. (For, with steel as the subject, Steve Dangos's situation is very much that of the celebrated "melting pot.") Also, the lengthy completed film was unsympathetically cut down without Vidor's permission or even knowledge. Given these facts, *An American Romance* is at least better than one might expect, although rather naive about labour relations. Visually, it glories in some fine colour scenes of furnaces and factories and fields.

THE PEOPLE IN THE CROWD

If King Vidor had made nothing but *The Crowd* (1928) he would still be assured of filmic immortality. It is a work of great beauty and true simplicity—in my opinion, one of three master-

James Murray and Eleanor Boardman in THE CROWD

pieces with which the silent cinema came to maturity and bravely met a premature end at one and the same time. (The other films I think of are Murnau's *Sunrise* and Dovzhenko's *Earth*). Of course, Vidor could never have directed such a film if he *had* made nothing else! Its simplicity is achieved by knowledge, not luck or artistic innocence. Its rare human truth counters the numerous evasions and half-truths with which Vidor, like all Hollywood directors (and not only Hollywood directors) has had to battle and compromise and contend. Parts of *The Crowd* have a bravura technique. The celebrated early scene can be quoted in which the camera glides up a huge office building and into the window of an enormous room, over the tops of many desks eventually to "discover" the average hero (James Murray) conscientiously at work amidst a sea of anonymity. Billy Wilder borrowed this idea (with acknowledgement) for the introduction of Jack Lemmon in *The Apartment* (1960) and the tribute involved is moving, for Wilder is not normally a director obliged to lift from anyone else. In later scenes, *The Crowd*'s visual style is a positive anticipation of the French "New Wave" with the camera virtuoso and, in the nicest sense, a *voyeur* roaming the streets, on open-top buses and in an amusement park, quite alien to the studio-bound conventions of its time.

Yet one remembers *The Crowd* for its apparent lack of "technique" rather than for its actual cleverness. It seems simply to *be* the story of a likeable, unremarkable young couple in urban America. Had *The Crowd* not been selected for a very apt and reverberant title, the film might well have gone by a name later used in Britain, *Millions Like Us*. The main drama in the film involves the hero's loss of his job and subsequent despondency and despair. Helped by his wife's love and patience, he finds the courage to continue. The ending is "happy" only to a point. (I speak of "the" ending with caution, because several were filmed and tried out, so that surviving copies of the film may vary). The husband has found only a subsistence-level job as a sandwichman and his celebration with his wife is a visit to a vaudeville theatre. As they laugh at the antics of a clown, the camera pulls back from the two in their seats, revealing a large audience, unknown to us or each other, all people in the crowd. The fact that Vidor had to fight to retain this ending, rather than having the husband become a millionaire or President or something, says much about Hollywood standards at the time. Certainly it is ironic, could be construed negatively and relates to the movies' use as an opiate to the public. But such thoughts about it would come only long after the fade-out. In terms of the plot and characters it is a joyously upbeat ending, carrying a delightful unexpected rightness. John and Mary (as in *Our Daily Bread* the young couple are named John and Mary Sims) find they can laugh and others will laugh with them.

Vidor's outlook in *The Crowd* fairly represents his guidance of "Everyman" through all his social pictures. He is concerned for him, understanding of his problems yet cautiously optimistic for the future. The extremes of pain that may be thought inherent in his situation are avoided by Vidor, here as in *The Big Parade*. Essentially his "Mr. Anyman" has modest aims and will not make trouble for the social system. He wants to better himself, look after his family, help his friends and get a good night's sleep.

There are, however, other leading characters in Vidor films who are not "Mr. Anyman" but very much "Mr. Somebody". These men have some standing, some position in the community and they have a responsibility, the director makes clear, to use their influence well and wisely. Thus, Robert Donat's Doctor Andrew Manson in *The Citadel* (1938). He begins in dire financial straits, no better than John and Mary, as assistant to a doctor in a Welsh mining village, suspected by his patients and half-starved by the doctor's shrewish wife (a great supporting performance, incidentally, by an unsung actress, Dilys Davis). Unable to pursue his own modern methods, he leaves for London and becomes a prosperous but essentially parasitic specialist, feeding off lonely widows and unsatisfied rich girls. Only when his conscience is jolted by events including the death of his best friend at the hands of an incompetent but highly paid quack does Manson return to medicine with a purpose—and gets scolded by the medical establishment for his pains. Manson is a figure close to Vidor's heart. The plot I have described is, of course, that of the novel's author, A. J. Cronin. It clearly fitted Vidor's ideas and sympathies, though, with the result that *The Citadel* remains a very moving and perceptive film, in spite of some plot contrivances and a slightly too moralistic tone in the context of today.

About another Vidor man of standing it is difficult to make a statement because of the scripting idiocies of *The Fountainhead* (1949). Vidor is not without reservation an Ayn Rand supporter and he disapproved of Gary Cooper blowing up a building because it hadn't been built his way! *The Fountainhead* was a commissioned film (from Warner Bros.). Perhaps *The Citadel* was no less commissioned but the difference in Vidor's involvement between the two pictures speaks volumes. He is a director, however, who always connects somewhere with his material. In so far as the story allows, Cooper's architect emerges as more concerned with his responsibility to human progress than to aesthetics or personal, superman, pique. It is a rather neat job of sabotaging Ayn Rand, though nobody said so at the time.

The "Mr. Somebody" of greatest substance in Vidor's work is surely Spencer Tracy in *Northwest Passage* (1939). As played by Tracy, Major Rogers is a figure of immense authority. He is also extremely likeable but here I have to stress "as played by Tracy". The characterisation of the martinet Rogers sees Vidor's liking of

Spencer Tracy as Major Rogers in NORTHWEST PASSAGE

a leader come uncomfortably close to submerging "the people in the crowd." In history, Rogers' Rangers must have been a rough-and-ready lot but in the picture they seldom argue Tracy's decisions—and then very democratically—and they never desert, unless they have gone out of their heads. It also sits more than a trifle uneasily today that Tracy and his submissive band attack and burn a sleeping Indian village. The tribe has massacred and outraged, we are told, but we have not *seen* them do anything wrong and they are certainly not belligerent in their sleep. Perhaps this is a plot weakness only, perhaps I should not berate Vidor for the conventions of good guys and bad guys in adventure movies. But I am still somewhat bothered by Major Rogers, who, beneath Tracy's charm, is something of a bastard. When the Indian village is destroyed by his men, Rogers reminds his men to kill only the bad Indians, not the good ones who, conveniently, wear white crosses on their backs. Perhaps in 1939 one could question less the morality and the smooth practicality of such discrimination.

In Vidor's work, quite often the leader and the crowd are in opposition, as well they might be. He tends to show sympathy for the crowd even though the leader is a hero and a big star. A quietly stunning moment occurs in *Northwest Passage* when Tracy is making morale-boosting jokes at a time of danger. We see one soldier laugh dutifully, then register private fear as the laugh freezes on his face. The Rogers character himself at one moment shows a recognition of the crowd and perhaps a secret desire to return to its ranks. Walter Brennan tells Tracy he is always right and it isn't good for a man to be always right. Tracy replies that at this time he is not a man but a soldier in command of men. "If you ever meet me as just a man, you may need a little charity." I suspect that Vidor would have made something from Rogers' degeneration in the later part of the story. But the continuation of *Northwest Passage* was never made.

WOMAN, WAKE UP

The title of a Florence Vidor movie can lead us into some thoughts on the women in King Vidor's films. (It should also be acceptable to both supporters and opponents of the women's liberation movement, being capable of more than one interpretation). Unlike George Cukor, for example, Vidor is not considered a "woman's director." Yet many of his films have centred on female characters and his work with actresses has been remarkable. Besides the several films with Florence Vidor and Eleanor Board-

man, he has directed Lillian Gish in *La Boheme,* Barbara Stan-
wyck in *Stella Dallas,* Margaret Sullavan, Hedy Lamarr, Kay
Francis, Audrey Hepburn—all to good avail. His comedies with
Marion Davies show exemplary understanding of her small but
decided talent. In fact, recent archive revivals of *The Patsy* and
Show People have been mainly responsible for us ceasing to think
of Marion Davies as merely the mistress of William Randolph
Hearst.

Apart from the Mary characters in *The Crowd* and *Our Daily
Bread,* Vidor's ladies are not, or seldom, "Everywoman." They
are more forceful and individual than that and, compared to "Mr.
Anyman," they are inclined to behave selfishly or at least oddly.
Stella Dallas doesn't try to better herself and her daughter in typical Vidor fashion. She goes in for self-denial and anonymous
assistance of the child, which is quite another matter! But at least
Stella's motives are above reproach. Some later Vidor heroines
are out for themselves alone. The director got into critical trouble
because of Pearl Chavez, Rosa Moline and Ruby Gentry.

These ladies are the stormy, not to say thunderous, heroines
of *Duel in the Sun, Beyond the Forest* and *Ruby Gentry.* From
another angle, they are one layer of Bette Davis between two
slices of Jennifer Jones. This bizarre sandwich-trilogy of post-war
films provides the main evidence for those several critics who
have neatly divided Vidor's career into two conflicting parts. Generally, according to this theory, the earlier work is much pre-
ferred—a line of optimistic, socially responsible pictures, abruptly
broken by a descent into lurid emotions and monstrous melodrama. Some writers, especially latterly, prefer the Vidor of
Ruby Gentry to the Vidor of *The Big Parade,* finding more vi-
tality and passion there but generally the director has disconcerted
admirers of his earlier work by the change in material and style.
Ironically, he himself is unhappy with *Lightning Strikes Twice*

(1951) on the grounds that it is a weak story. Nobody has called it his best film but nobody else has worried about it either. It is the strength, not the weakness, of his later films that has sounded an alarm.

How true is this division in Vidor's career? Nothing is quite so neat and tidy. Back in 1930 Vidor and Thalberg wondered whether *Billy the Kid* was going to prove too violent. Its mayhem (sadly unavailable for viewing today) comes between *The Crowd* and *Our Daily Bread*. Similarly, immediately before *Ruby Gentry,* Vidor made *Japanese War Bride,* which is a film of concern for ordinary people once again (although thwarted by heavy-handed plotting). We must admit to such kinks in the time-scheme of Vidor's work. Having done so, we must also admit some validity to the early-late judgement. Why? What happened?

One important thing that happened was the failure of *An American Romance* in 1944. Vidor had his heart very strongly in his "steel" film. He was saddened at having Brian Donlevy in place of Spencer Tracy and he was incensed by the studio's secretive and brutal cutting of the film for release. He left M-G-M for ever, after having helped to build it from the small Metro company to the giant of Hollywood. For two years he made no films. When he returned to work, it was for David O. Selznick on *Duel in the Sun.*

Selznick, it has often been noted, spent the rest of his life after 1939 trying to "top" *Gone with the Wind.* His choice of a western adventure scripted by himself from another best-selling grandiose novel was to prove his most energetic attempt at upstaging his own previous achievement. He failed, of course, but he tried very hard. Selznick's choice of director for *Duel in the Sun* was crucial and it must have helped Vidor's prestige in the industry—and probably his own self-esteem—to be so chosen at that difficult point in his career. There was a price tag, naturally. Selznick had not only written the screenplay for *Duel in the Sun*: he was determined virtually to direct it himself. All camera angles, movements and lighting arrangements had to be approved by the producer who was constantly present on the set. In addition, his control over Jennifer Jones's every flick of eyelash is legendary. Obviously the genesis of a "new Vidor" is bound up with the creativity, for better or worse, of Selznick. Strangely enough, Selznick was also doing something different from his earlier work. They were changing times.

Vidor had many arguments with Selznick during shooting and finally quit before the end. Several other directors worked on the massive film (William Dieterle most extensively) both before and after his departure. Some of it *looks* like Vidor but it is hard to evaluate his precise contribution because the overall visual concept is *Gone with the Wind* revisited—and did anyone but Selznick really "direct" that? The glaring latter-day development of *Duel* from *GWTW*, however, is its total lack of artistic discretion. The medium-rare sunsets of 1939 have become raw and bleeding red. Jones's half-caste, trouble-making girl is without any of the finesse or style with which Scarlett O'Hara sugared the pill of ruining people's lives. Rhett Butler would never have wrecked a train as Gregory Peck's Lewt McCanles does. (Even the names are outsize in *Duel in the Sun*). Vidor disliked this plot point particularly and fought, in vain, to change it, as later he would with the architect's destruction of his building in *The Fountainhead*. Whatever the emotional charge in these later films, he seems never to have acquired a taste for explosives.

It will be fairer to look for the "new" Vidor in the films following *Duel in the Sun*, although the fact of its commercial success (less than *GWTW* but still very healthy) should not be discounted as an influence. He worked next for a less egotistical producer, the respected Henry Blanke at Warner Bros., and then became his own producer on two films in partnership with Joseph Bernhard. Here he would have had greater freedom than with Selznick. Greater freedom, not total freedom: let us remember that.

Both *Beyond the Forest* (1949) and *Ruby Gentry* (1952) are ultimately in line with Vidor's other, "purer" work. In each film, the selfish, headstrong heroine is not, intrinsically, likeable and moreover is presented with a viable alternative to her neurosis in a calmer, saner way of life. Significantly, neither Ruby Gentry nor Rosa Moline has much fun from philandering! Of the two films, *Ruby Gentry* has been more noted but *Beyond the Forest* seems to me the stronger—partly because of a greater conviction in Vidor's visual response, partly because Bette Davis is simply a more compelling actress than Jennifer Jones, even when on the verge of grotesquerie with aggressive eyes and a black fright wig. As a result, I will base my comments here on *Beyond the Forest.*

After the credit titles, and Max Steiner's moody music, the film begins with a "creeper" title, expounding the virtues of morality in rather flowery language and suggesting that it is good "to look on the face of evil once in a while." This disclaimer, before scenes of relative salaciousness, has a familiar Hollywood ring and might be looked on merely as a device to placate pressure groups. In the context of what follows, however, one simple and vital fact emerges clearly. Vidor believes the statement. Rosa Moline could—should—be happy in her small-town, midwestern world, Vidor suggests. The opening images, shot on location, make up a very clever and touching assembly of views. This is a mill town, yet close to idyllic America. Soon after, Rosa is seen with her doctor husband (Joseph Cotten). He is fishing in the river while Rosa watches, bored. The camera tracks along the river bank, viewing Cotten in the shining water through foliage and trees which pass in foreground before the lens. All this is quietly beau-

Above, guns at the ready: Jennifer Jones in DUEL IN THE SUN (left) and RUBY GENTRY. Below, "What a dump": Bette Davis as Rosa with Minor Watson in BEYOND THE FOREST

tiful and serene. A man—or a woman—might be happy here. But not Rosa.

Rosa wants Chicago. She wants it, not in some vague sense of spiritual longing, not as Chekhov's Three Sisters want Moscow, but to be clothed in the "New Look" and kept by her lover (David Brian). In fact, she gets to the city but only to be rebuffed and humiliated. A second attempt to go there, while she is weak and ill, ends in her death by the tracks, just yards from the outgoing train. (This is a purely visual conclusion, reminiscent of a silent film and not only because Davis's makeup gives her a strange hint of Lillian Gish—a fallen Lillian Gish figure, battling fruitlessly for her mistaken choice of life style).

For all its late Forties, *film noir* ambience, then, *Beyond the Forest* does conform to much of mainstream Vidor. The style prevailing during any period of movie history exacts some compliance from almost any artist. I think of Frank Borzage's *Moonrise* (also 1949), with its murders and foreboding, a much darker film than any by Borzage in earlier years (*Seventh Heaven, Little Man, What Now?*) and yet still essentially a Borzage romance. Similarly, *Beyond the Forest*. Two scenes when plot situations have an unexpected closeness evoke, of all unlikely pictures, memories of *The Citadel*. Rosa's husband delivers a baby in difficult conditions; the images resemble those of Robert Donat's Doctor Manson, eleven years removed—eleven years and apparently an entire world of sentiment and feeling. A woman prays for the child and the doctor's shadow is seen on the wall. Later, when Rosa is on her abortive pleasure trip to Chicago, she wanders helplessly through the unfriendly night. Doctor Manson had similarly wandered through London, while at low ebb in his personal and ideological life. In both instances, the city is dark indeed. In London, fog; in Chicago, rain. And in both instances drunkenness—whether in English pub or American bar—is Vidor's symbol for failure, disappointment, defeat. Rosa and Manson are not drunk but drunkenness is around them, in an almost Dickensian squalor of mean streets and low lighting. In *The Citadel* Manson is only temporarily swayed from his vocation. Rosa, with no vocation, is more seriously lost. The degrees of despair differ but the visual language is the same. (Incidentally, Bette Davis pronounces the famous line, "What a dump," quickly and quietly—not at all like the ultra-Davis impersonation by Elizabeth Taylor in *Who's Afraid of Virginia Woolf?*) A further identification with earlier Vidor in this regard comes from the character of the bad black girl in *Hallelujah*. As described in plot synopses, she seems just as selfish and unreliable to men as any of the later ladies. (But I must resort to second-hand reports on her as, regrettably, I have never yet managed to see *Hallelujah* which is obviously an important film in Vidor's career.)

A TREE IS A TREE

King Vidor titled his autobiography (published in 1953) "A Tree Is A Tree." This sounds properly solid and of the earth to represent his work; truly, he has used trees very knowingly and lovingly both as beautiful objects and as symbols of the natural world. Many an actress has been pictured by Vidor between branches or under blossom. But the title involves irony and an awareness of the illusion—sometimes even the deceit—implicit in making movies. Abe Stern, a producer in the early days, objected to the expense and bother of location filming. He asked what was the need to travel and he asked it rhetorically, with the purse strings in his hands. "A rock is a rock and a tree is a tree. Shoot it in Griffith Park!"

Vidor has, on occasion, worked in Griffith Park. This Los Angeles land for all seasons stood in, credibly, for France in parts of *The Big Parade*. On certain films, however, he has travelled fur-

ther afield to much wider open spaces with immeasurably fine results. *Northwest Passage*, for example, gains greatly from its filming around Lake Payette, Idaho. Not that the story takes place
in Idaho but in New York State and Canada! Even so, Lake Payette is considerably more wild and rugged and "authentic" than
good old Griffith Park. With this location advantage, and with
softly glowing 1940 Technicolor, *Northwest Passage* contains some
of Vidor's finest images and well illustrates the straightforward
yet imaginative nature of his camera style. The agreeable softness
of colour tones in the film would be rarely seen in later Hollywood pictures, when the trend towards a harder, more glaring
look spread from the Technicolor musicals at Fox. The settings
and costumes of Kenneth Roberts's adventure story lend themselves entirely to muted shades—the varied greens and browns of
growing things, the quiet blue of sky and river. To these are
added the deep green uniforms of Rogers' Rangers. By deliberate
contrast, the red-coated British soldiers in marching formation
have a thrilling visual impact but even their coats do not shout
with the redness of mail boxes.

The single most outstanding shot in *Northwest Passage* has
the beauty of an individual painting and yet contributes, as it
must to be successful, to the atmosphere and movement of the
entire film. The Rangers are passing silently and dangerously by
an Indian village as they canoe along the river. It is night and
the screen is almost black. All we see, on one thin upright strip
of the screen is a camp fire glowing and the flames' reflection in
the placid water. A tiny moment in a two-hour film yet as memorable as the great scene where the Rangers have to cross a now
turbulent river, which they do by forming a human chain, man
by man, across the torrent. This set-piece is painful as well as
exciting, largely because it is real. The players endured hardship in a
context where "Griffith Park" would not have passed muster.

Like many Vidor films, *Northwest Passage* relies very little on moving camerawork—surprisingly little, since this is the story of a long cross-country trek. The forward movement, the pulse of the adventure, is maintained instead by keeping the group of Rangers massed together and either advancing towards the camera or departing from it. It is characteristic of Vidor that most of the important action is arranged to happen before the camera, which *records* more than takes part in. The most noticeable camera movements in this film occur, endearingly, when it is necessary to keep sight of Tracy's Major Rogers! He has a habit of pacing quickly up and down in front of his men, while thinking out and instructing them in spurts on the next course of action.

A crucial use of composition, a reliance on the power of the picture frame, is a mark of many fine directors who began their careers in the silent period. (Henry King, for example, very much fits the pattern, as does John Ford.) If we turn to a silent film by Vidor we will see the visual style already well established in 1926, with *La Boheme*. In trying to *look at* a film, there is something to be said for choosing one without extraordinary subject matter. Without slighting the love of Rodolphe and Mimi, their story is simple compared to those, backed by social forces, of *The Big Parade* and *The Crowd*. How does Vidor treat his "Scenes de la Vie de Boheme"?

He treats them with wit and charm and an agreeable Gallic lightness, offering a nice alternative to the heavier romantic emphasis of Puccini's opera. A surprising amount of the film is played in comedy vein, with Lillian Gish even acting as foil to John Gilbert at moments, such as when Rodolphe acts out the play he has written and Mimi reacts in muted wonderment. The lovers' first meeting is delayed until after several scenes of fooling between the artist friends. Yet sufficient seriousness is established from the beginning to allow a gradual dramatic curve to sadness, with Mimi's illness and death. And, although this is no social document, the film makes clear that poverty and injustice lie behind all that picturesque starving in garrets which is often, from afar, considered so attractive. The first, unforgettable, shot of Mimi shows her as a tiny figure at the end of a long, low attic room, working at her embroidery by which she makes a frugal living. She is the very picture of vulnerability. Vidor likes to use such distant placing of a character and in *La Boheme* he has deep sets to add to the impact. Gilbert's romantic writer is seen at his desk way beyond the antics of his more frivolous friends, in a physical as well as a mental sense.

John Gilbert and Lillian Gish in LA BOHEME

At the heart of *La Boheme* is a beautiful scene of a picnic in the country, at which Mimi first confesses her love for Rodolphe. In exhilaration, they run and dance under the summer trees of a beautiful landscape. (Griffith Park? It could be!) For Miss Gish, a tree can be more than a tree; it can also be a useful obstacle. She had considerable control over her M-G-M films and it had been her idea that Mimi and Rodolphe should not be seen kissing or even touching each other. She was not able to keep this distance in all scenes. Vidor eventually supported her idea but studio executives did not. There remains a scene in which they kiss against a window pane and in the picnic sequence Lillian/Mimi finds tree trunks useful barriers to the ardour of Gilbert/Rodolphe. When she was overruled about a *complete* lack of physical contact, it is perhaps significant that the strong-willed Miss Gish initiates the kissing scene by making the first move herself.

I have re-seen *La Boheme* since writing the earlier lines about *Northwest Passage* and find my comments about Vidor's limited use of camera movement rather startlingly confirmed. When the lovers run and dance in the picnic scene, Vidor's camera moves and even gently sways with them, to great effect. But this scene comes midway through the film and there has been *no camera movement at all* to this point. I doubt if anyone would be aware of this without keeping both eyes peeled; the film does not suffer from a static feeling, because of the life and motion within each shot, but this is a useful reminder that not all silent cinema was Murnau and Gance and the camera pyrotechnics of *Sunrise* and *Napoleon*.

WAR AND PEACE

In 1956 King Vidor made *War and Peace* and in 1959 *Solomon and Sheba*. The choice of such spectacular subjects mirrors that age—a period of "roadshow attractions," the Bible, battles

Even in 1956, Vidor uses the megaphone: directing Audrey
Hepburn and Henry Fonda in WAR AND PEACE

and ancient romance. Unfortunately, the usual critical suspicion
of such films has left *War and Peace* badly underrated. It is one
of the director's finest works—an intelligent, exciting and moving
distillation of its great source material in Tolstoy. It, rather than
Solomon and Sheba, stands as a worthy summation of Vidor's significant career. The latter film was shadowed by tragedy in that
Tyrone Power, playing Solomon, died suddenly during production. He was replaced by Yul Brynner. Vidor told me of a feeling
of utter dejection when he realised the necessity of all the added
shooting in an atmosphere saddened by the death and, obviously,
under greater pressure of budgets and temperaments. An added
irony is that, had the battle and crowd scenes been scheduled for

filming *after* the character footage, Power would probably have lived to complete his role. But they were shot first and some moments of visual splendour from them are all that are really memorable from this unhappy venture.

The Italian Tolstoy production is another matter. After "War, Wheat and Steel"—*War and Peace*. A chance, indeed, for a director to spread his wings. There are moments in the first part of the film which leave room for doubt that the massive enterprise will work. Though the scripting is generally clean and clear, it does fall prey here and there to the dangers of compressed exposition. "I believe that's my friend Prince Andrey Bolkonsky. May I bring him over?" Or, "I came to say goodbye, I'm leaving Moscow tomorrow." That sort of thing. But there are great compensations, such as the beautiful scene where Pierre (Henry Fonda) talks of life to Natasha (Audrey Hepburn) as she sits under the shade of great trees and sketches a colt frisking in the field— a young thing like herself on the threshold of leaping life. (A strangely international scene, incidentally, in visual terms, shot in Italy, standing in acceptably for Russia yet warmly American in its framing.) And, from the Battle of Borodino to the end, the film exhibits a fine frenzied spirit of pace and precision as one splendidly realised scene follows another. The battle itself; the scene of Natasha and her family packing up to leave Moscow, in which the impulsive kindness of their flinging out furniture from the carts to make room for wounded soldiers finds an obviously delighted response from Vidor (I think he would have done the same thing himself); the staggering, ragged march of Napoleon's defeated army through the snow and biting cold of Russian winter, in unforgettable scenes with a kind of frozen colour where even the trees on the landscape are, for once in Vidor, gaunt and gravely menacing.

Unusually for such super-productions, Vidor personally shot

the main spectacular scene in *War and Peace,* rather than leave it to a second unit director. The Battle of Borodino is a magnificent set piece, yet it begins with deceptive quietness and here Vidor does rely heavily on camera movement. In fact, he introduces the action with one of the most subtly encompassing moving shots in film history. The spiritually questing Pierre has come to view the fighting. Before he can condemn war, he feels he has to see it. We see Pierre on a verdant country road. It is a lovely summer day; he picks a sunflower. The camera follows him as he climbs a ridge—and there is the battle, war violating peace as soldiers run and ride and fight on different levels in a great valley receding far beyond Pierre. He stands transfixed and drops the flower. Having experienced this sensation with a leading character, the audience is now ready to see a battle as something more than the usual knockabout action and Vidor supplies images that invoke terror and pity as well as the inevitable superficial sense of thrill. One image may be cited to stand for many, as a troop of cavalry rides from the left of the screen through a crowd of foot soldiers marching from the right.

War is easier to put into pictures than peace. One of Vidor's means of conveying a peaceful emotion is, as already suggested, natural outdoor beauty. The other is Audrey Hepburn, whose wonderfully played Natasha is a consoling force to all around her. The wounded Andrey (Mel Ferrer) sees her outlined in a dark doorway. She seems an angel, a young mother, a nurse. Near the end of the film, when her family returns to a stricken home, Natasha is there, cheering everyone up though full of grave doubts herself before the final meeting with Pierre. Vidor and Miss Hepburn worked together at precisely the right moment and entirely deserved each other.

Hepburn as Natasha in WAR AND PEACE

A LETTER FROM KING VIDOR

In February 1973, Mr. Vidor very kindly (and forthrightly) answered certain questions about his career. While writing this essay I re-saw *The Wizard of Oz* and the experience reminded me of a rumour that I had once heard but since forgotten to the effect that Vidor had done some shooting on this production. The framing scenes to the fantasy, set in Kansas, and not in colour, had the *look* of Vidor quite strongly, especially the approach of the cyclone (shades of Galveston, 1913!) with shots of horses rearing and breaking loose in fright and the homely image of Auntie Em standing anxiously by the farmhouse door.

"When Victor Fleming, who directed most of *The Wizard of Oz* and who received credit as the director, had the opportunity to direct *Gone with the Wind,* he was about three weeks from finishing *The Wizard of Oz.* David Selznick, who had also talked to me about taking over *Gone with the Wind* after Cukor was leaving the film, asked me if I would be willing to take over the remaining part of *The Wizard of Oz* if Fleming would come and undertake *Gone with the Wind.* Strange as it may seem, to me the script of *Gone with the Wind* needed so much work that I was glad to do *The Wizard of Oz* rather than *Gone with the Wind.* I spent one day with Fleming in the studio going around and looking at sets that hadn't been used. Fleming left after one day and I took over the film.

"I do remember that I shot the scene with the very popular song, 'Somewhere Over the Rainbow.' I also remember shooting the scenes in the house during the cyclone and many of the Kansas scenes. I don't exactly remember at this moment how many or what part. I worked with Ray Bolger, Jack Haley and Bert Lahr, and with Frank Morgan who was playing the wizard. I remember shooting scenes of the three characters mentioned singing the song, 'We're Off to See the Wizard.' Each year when the perennial favourite *Wizard of Oz* is shown and I hear Judy Garland singing 'Somewhere Over the Rainbow' I get a tremendous kick knowing that I shot the scenes, or whenever I hear the record played I remember that I was in on the beginning. I had very much the feeling of adapting the movement of silent films to the staging of a musical number. Previously in most of the sound musicals someone stood up in front of the camera and sang directly to the camera. In directing 'Somewhere Over the Rainbow' I was able to keep the movement of Judy Garland flowing freely very much in the style of a silent scene. I didn't ask for credit on the film and I did not want it. The Director's Guild, of which I was first President (and probably I was on the board at that time), was very much in the mood to give credit to only one director on a film and mainly this is the director who plans the film in advance and picks the locations and supervises the settings, the costumes and casting, and I never have believed—and the Director's Guild felt—that any director coming in and taking over should get credit in any way equivalent with the director who inaugurated the whole project."

The reference to co-direction credits has obvious bearing on Vidor's successful attempts to retain sole direction billing on *Duel in the Sun*. However, on another film, *A Miracle Can Happen,* there was less arguable sharing of credits, this being an episode story. My enquiry about this quite minor film was mainly "for the record" but produced an unexpectedly interesting piece of information.

"As to *A Miracle Can Happen,* I directed two episodes, taking about two weeks for each one. The first was with Burgess Meredith and Charles Laughton. As I remember, the story concerned Meredith going out and interviewing people for something he was writing. Laughton played the part of a minister, and in the episode, he gave one of his famous interpretations of a Bible story. He had done this, I believe, touring the country and that was why it was worked into the film. When the picture was previewed, it was done with a laugh meter or rather with the audience registering their impressions on some sort of moving tape. The Laughton episode being a dramatic one, there were very few laugh indications on the tape. The overall objective of the film was to be a comedy. The Laughton episode was dropped, and originally it was intended to make an entire film out of this one episode. This was talked of many times but never accomplished.

"The second episode was with Burgess Meredith and Paulette Goddard and concerned itself with their relationship and Meredith's going out to do the interviews. In other words, the framing part of the film.

"I felt that the Laughton episode was most effective and thought it was absolutely ridiculous that it was not included in the film. It would have given a good rest from the expected laughter and contrast always helps both the comedy and dramatic effect.

"As to *The Big Parade* there were no two-colour Technicolor scenes. [American Film Institute reference material has stated otherwise—C.D.] There could have been some tinted scenes. This was a process that we used in early films for night scenes and for fire scenes. Night scenes were tinted blue, particularly when they were shot in the day time, but I do not recall whether any tinting was done in *The Big Parade*, certainly no Technicolor.

"The third question about the change in my style after the Second World War, my career was designed somewhat along the line that in order to make the films that were closest to my heart one might say came from one's own inside—in other words the *auteur* theory—I must keep up my box-office name in order to be permitted to do the stories and films which were not obviously box-office. Sometimes these consciously box-office films didn't work out that way and sometimes the more personal statements turned out to be good box-office. *Duel in the Sun* was originally to be a personal film and one that I thought would be a very moody and simple statement about the basic story. But Mr. Selznick was a very dominant factor as a producer and a writer and when he began to see the possibilities of the film he dropped other projects upon which he was working and concentrated all of his efforts on *Duel*. This involved a general blowing up or expanding process modelled somewhat after *Gone with the Wind*. Selznick was one of the few producers who was capable of dominating the film, in fact, I don't know of any other who so completely impregnated the film throughout with his own ideas and personality. However, he did not participate except through his wife, Jennifer Jones, in the making of the film *Ruby Gentry*. This film was chosen and done in the manner it was because at that time I was producing films under a small independent set-up and I wanted our efforts and our company to be successful.

"An independent company not working under the umbrella of a large distributing company or a large studio has a much tougher battle. They could ignore the individual film quite easily so, therefore, we had to have in it probably more box-office consciousness and more popular appeal than I would have had in some of my other films. I saw *Ruby Gentry* recently and I feel rather good about it, certainly I have no apologies to make for it. For example, take the situation today of Francis Ford Coppola. He told me two years ago that he was finished with Hollywood and was working and living in San Francisco and the next thing you know he makes the all time box-office top film *The Godfather* and now he can possibly make anything he wants to. If you follow the careers of many directors I think you will find somewhat the pattern of which I speak."

King Vidor Filmography

Some details of his earlier short films made in Texas and California are given in the essay. Slight confusion has arisen in the past because of the director's involvement with Florence Vidor Productions. King Vidor is credited as "presenting" *Alice Adams* (1923, Rowland V. Lee). He is not, apparently, credited on *Woman, Wake Up!* (1922, Marcus Harrison) although the film is copyright in his name. Both these titles have usually been included in lists of Vidor's directed work.

King Vidor has made two brief appearances as "himself" in Hollywood-set pictures. He and Florence Vidor, along with many other celebrities, were seen in *Souls for Sale* (1923, Rupert Hughes). In *It's a Great Feeling* (1949, David Butler), King Vidor is one of the Warner contract directors who, for plot purposes, refuse to direct ham actor Jack Carson. He also played a chauffeur in *The Intrigue* (1916, Frank Lloyd).

With regard to King W. Vidor Productions, the middle initial stands for Wallis.

SHORT FILMS:

Documentaries
Hurricane in Galveston (1913, King Vidor, Roy Clough). Also co-producer.
Military Parade in Galveston (1913, King Vidor). Newsreel.
Sugar Manufacture (1914, King Vidor). Florence Arto appeared in some scenes.
Fort Worth Robbery (1915, King Vidor). Also producer and actor.
Actualities filmed from train between Galveston and Fort Worth (1915, King Vidor). Series of twenty films on child education (1918, King Vidor). Three of these thirty minute films, produced, written by and featuring Judge William Brown were strung together and released as a feature. The probable titles were *Danny Asks Why; The Demand of Dugan* and *Gumdrops and Overalls*.

IN TOW (1914). Comedy. *Sc:* King Vidor. *Ph:* John Boggs. *With* King Vidor. *Prod:* King Vidor for Vidor. 20 m.
TWO COMEDIES (?) (1914). *Dir:* Edward Sedgwick. *Sc:* King Vidor, Edward Sedgwick. *Tech. Asst:* King Vidor. *With* King Vidor, Edward Sedgwick. *Prod:* King Vidor for UP. 10 m. each.
WHEN IT RAINS, IT POURS (1916). Plot unknown, probably comedy. *Sc:* King Vidor. *Prod:* William Wolbert for Vitagraph Company of America. 10 m.
WHAT'LL WE DO WITH UNCLE? (1917). Plot unknown, probably comedy. *Dir:* William Beaudine. *Sc:* King Vidor. *Prod:* Universal/Victor. 10 m.
A BAD LITTLE GOOD MAN (1917). Plot unknown. *Dir:* William Beaudine. *Sc:* King Vidor. *Prod:* Universal/Nestor. 10 m.

FEATURES:

THE TURN IN THE ROAD (1919). "Christian Science" drama of a man's faith and doubt. *Sc:* King Vidor. *With* Helen Jerome Eddy (*June Barker*), Lloyd Hughes (*Paul Perry*), George Nichols (*Hamilton Perry*), Ben Alexander (*Bob*), Pauline Curley, Winter Hall. *Prod:* Brent-

wood Film Corp./Robertson-Cole. 5 reels.
BETTER TIMES (1919). Romantic comedy about a "wallflower" who wins the love of a ball player. *Sc:* King Vidor. *With* ZaSu Pitts (*Nancy Scroogs*), David Butler (*Peter*), Jack MacDonald (*Ezra Scroogs*). *Prod:* Brentwood Film Corp./ Robertson-Cole. 5 reels.

THE OTHER HALF (1919). First World War veteran returns full of hope for reconciliation of the social classes, but soon follows in the moneymaking footsteps of his deceased businessman father, causing his *fiancée* to break off the engagement and to start up a radical newspaper; an action that eventually brings the two lovers together again. *Sc:* King Vidor. *With* Florence Vidor (*Katherine Boone*), Charles Meredith (*Donald Trent*), ZaSu Pitts (*The Jazz Kid*), David Butler (*Corporal Jimmy*), Thomas Jefferson. Alfred Allen, Frances Raymond, Hugh Saxon, Arthur Redden. *Prod:* Brentwood Film Corp./Robertson-Cole. 5 reels.

POOR RELATIONS (1919). The village grocer's daughter qualifies as an architect, and meets a rich heir when she is designing a golf-course clubhouse. *Sc:* King Vidor (from his own play). *With* Florence Vidor (*Dorothy Perkins*), William Du Vaull (*Pa Perkins*), ZaSu Pitts (*Daisy Perkins*), Charles Meredith (*Monte Rhodes*), Lilian Leighton, Roscoe Karns. *Prod:* Brentwood Film Corp./ Robertson-Cole. 5 reels.

THE JACK-KNIFE MAN (1920). Story of shanty boatmen on the Mississippi. *Sc:* William Parker, King Vidor (novel by Ellis Parker Butler). *With* Fred Turner (*Peter Lane*), Florence Vidor (*Mrs. Montgomery*), Harry Todd (*Booge*),

Claire McDowell, Bobby Kelso, Willis Marks, Lilian Leighton, James Corrigan, Charles Arling. *Prod:* King Vidor for First National. 6 reels.

THE FAMILY HONOR (1920). The heroine makes sacrifices to send her brother to college, but he emerges a wastrel and gambler, until he comes to his senses after being wrongfully suspected of a shooting. *Sc:* William Parker (a story by John Booth Harrower). *Ph:* Ira H. Morgan. *With* Florence Vidor (*Beverly Tucker*), Roscoe Karns (*Dal Tucker*), Ben Alexander (*Little Ben*), Charles Meredith (*Merle Curran*), George Nicholas, J. P. Lockney, Willis Marks, Harold Goodwin. *Prod:* King Vidor for First National. 5 reels.

THE SKY PILOT (1921). Romance of a young minister, with this nickname, in Canada's cattle country. *Sc:* John McDermott, Faith Green (novel by Ralph Connor). *Ph:* Gus Petersen. *With* John Bowers (*The Sky Pilot*), Colleen Moore (*Gwen*), David Butler (*Bill Hendricks*), Harry Todd (*The Old Timer*), James Corrigan, Donald MacDonald, Kathleen Kirkham. *Prod:* Cathrine Curtis for Cathrine Curtis Corporation/Associated First National. 7 reels.

LOVE NEVER DIES (1921). Domestic drama of parental and filial misunderstandings. *Sc:* King Vidor (novel "The Cottage of Delight" by William Nathaniel Harben). *Ph:* Max Dupont. *With* Lloyd Hughes (*John Trott*), Madge Bellamy (*Tilly Whaley*), Joe Bennett (*Joel Eperson*), Lilian Leighton (*Mrs. Cavanaugh*), Fred Gambold, Julia Brown, Frank Brownlee, Winifred Greenwood, Claire McDowell. *Prod:* King Vidor for King W. Vidor Productions/Associated

Producers. 7 reels.

THE REAL ADVENTURE (1922). Drama of a successful lady dress designer who settles for the "real adventure" of marriage. *Sc:* Mildred Considine (novel by Henry Kitchell Webster). *Ph:* George Barnes. *With* Florence Vidor (*Rose Stanton*), Clyde Fillmore (*Rodney Aldrich*), Nellie Peck Saunders (*Mrs. Stanton*), Lilyan McCarthy, Philip Ryder. *Prod:* Arthur S. Kane for Florence Vidor Productions-Cameo Pictures/Associated Exhibitors. 5 reels.

DUSK TO DAWN (1922). Fantasy of a girl's double life, waking and in dreams. *Sc:* Frank Howard Clark (novel "The Shuttle Soul" by Katherine Hill). *Ph:* George Barnes. *With* Florence Vidor (*Marjorie/Aziza*), Jack Mulhall (*Philip*), Truman Van Dyke (*Ralph*), James Neill (*John*), Lydia Knott, Herbert Fortier, Sidney Franklin, Norris Johnson, Nellie Anderson. *Prod:* King Vidor for Florence Vidor Productions/Associated Exhibitors. 6 reels.

CONQUERING THE WOMAN (1922). Drama of girl under spell of European "decadence" but who finds American true love. *Sc:* Frank Howard Clark (serial story of "Kidnapping Coline" by Henry Cottrell Rowland). *Ph:* George Barnes. *With* Florence Vidor (*Judith Stafford*), Bert Sprotte (*Tobias Stafford*), Mathilde Brundage (*Aunt Sophia*), David Butler (*Larry Saunders*), Roscoe Karns, Peter Burke, Harry Todd. *Prod:* King Vidor for King W. Vidor Productions/Associated Exhibitors. 6 reels.

PEG O' MY HEART (1922). Sentimental comedy-drama of high-style English life. *Sc:* Mary O'Hara (play by J. Hartley Manners). *Ph:* George Barnes. *With* Laurette Taylor (*Margaret 'Peg' O'Connell*), Mahlon Hamilton (*Sir Gerald Adair*), Russell Simpson (*Jim*), Ethel Grey Terry (*Ethel Chichester*), Nigel Barrie, Lionel Belmore, Vera Lewis, Sidna Beth Ivins, D.R.O. Hatswell, Aileen O'Malley, Fred Huntly, Michael a dog. *Prod:* (Under supervision of) J. Hartley Manners for Metro. 8 reels. Re-made 1933 (*dir:* Robert Z. Leonard).

THE WOMAN OF BRONZE (1923). Romantic drama, with slight "Pygmalion" overtones, of love between artist and model. *Sc:* Hope Loring, Louis Duryea Lighton (play by Henry Kistemaeckers). *Ph:* William O'Connell. *Art dir:* Joseph Wright. *With* Clara Kimball Young (*Vivian Hunt*), John Bowers (*Paddy Miles*), Kathryn McGuire (*Sylvia Morton*), Edwin Stevens, Lloyd Whitlock, Edward Kimball. *Prod:* Harry Garson for Samuel Zierler Photoplay/Metro. 6 reels.

THREE WISE FOOLS (1923). Three men become guardians of a young girl. *Sc:* King Vidor, June Mathis (adaptation by John McDermott, James O'Hanlon from play by Austin Strong, Winchell Smith). *Ph:* Charles Van Enger. *With* Eleanor Boardman (*Rena Fairchild/Sidney Fairchild*), Claude Gillingwater (*Theodore Findley*), William H. Crane (*Hon. James Trumbull*), Alec B. Francis (*Dr. Richard Gaunt*), John Sainpolis, Brinsley Shaw, Fred Esmelton, William Haines, Lucien Littlefield, ZaSu Pitts, Creighton Hale, Raymond Hatton, Martha Mattox, Fred J. Butler, Charles Hickman, Craig Biddle Jr. *Prod:* Goldwyn Pictures. 7 reels. Re-made 1946 (*dir:* Edward Buzzell).

WILD ORANGES (1924). Melodrama and romance, set on a remote island off

Georgia. *Sc:* King Vidor (novel by Joseph Hergesheimer). *Ph:* John W. Boyle. *With* Virginia Valli (*Nellie Stope*), Frank Mayo (*John Woolfolk*), Ford Sterling (*Paul Halvard*), Nigel De Brulier (*Lichfield Stope*), Charles A. Post. *Prod:* Goldwyn Pictures. 7 reels.

HAPPINESS (1924). Sentimental drama of friendship and philanthropy. *Sc:* J. Hartley Manners (his play). *Ph:* Chester A. Lyons. *With* Laurette Taylor (*Jenny Wreay*), Pat O'Malley (*Fermoy MacDonaugh*), Hedda Hopper (*Mrs. Chrystal Pole*), Cyril Chadwick (*Philip Chandos*), Edith Yorke, Patterson Dial, Joan Standing, Lawrence Grant, Charlotte Mineau. *Prod:* Metro Pictures. 8 reels.

WINE OF YOUTH (1924). Story of a girl who resists marriage—for a while. *Sc:* Carey Wilson (play "Mary the Third" by Rachel Crothers). *Ph:* John J. Mescall. *Art dir:* Charles L. Cadwallader. *Asst. dir:* David Howard. *With* Eleanor Boardman (*Mary*), Ben Lyon (*Lynn*), William Haines (*Hal*), William Collier Jr. (*Max*), Pauline Garon, Eulalie Jensen, E. J. Ratcliffe, Gertrude Claire, Robert Agnew, Lucille Hutton, Virginia Lee Corbin, Gloria Heller, Sidney De Grey. *Prod:* King Vidor for Metro-Goldwyn. 7 reels.

HIS HOUR (1924). High romance of Russian prince and English girl in Egypt and other places. *Sc:* Elinor Glyn (her novel). *Ph:* John Mescall. *Titles:* King Vidor, Maude Fulton. *Art dir:* Cedric Gibbons. *Cost:* Sophie Wachner. *Asst. dir:* David Howard. *With* Aileen Pringle (*Tamara Loraine*), John Gilbert (*Gritzko*), Emily Fitzroy (*Princess Ardacheff*), Mario Carillo (*Count Valonne*), Lawrence Grant (*Stephen Strong*), Dale Fuller (*Olga Gleboff*), George Wag-

goner, Bertram Grassby, Jacqueline Gadsdon, Carrie Clark Ward, Jill Reties, Wilfred Gough, Frederick Vroom, Mathilde Comont, E. Eliazaroff, David Mir, Bert Sprotte. *Prod:* (under supervision of) Elinor Glyn for Louis B. Mayer Productions/Metro-Goldwyn. 7 reels.

WIFE OF THE CENTAUR (1924). Drama about a novelist and his wavering from marriage. *Sc:* Douglas Z. Doty (novel by Cyril Hume). *Ph:* John Arnold. *Art dir:* Cedric Gibbons. *Cost:* Sophie Wachner. *Asst. dir:* David Howard. *Ed:* Hugh Wynn. *With* Eleanor Boardman (*Joan Converse*), John Gilbert (*Jeffrey Dwyer*), Aileen Pringle (*Inez Martin*), Kate Price (*Mattie*), Kate Lester (*Mrs. Converse*), William Haines, Bruce Covington, Philo McCullough, Jacqueline Gadsdon, Lincoln Stedman, William Orlamond. *Prod:* Metro-Goldwyn. 7 reels.

PROUD FLESH (1925). Comedy of a headstrong girl's romance. *Sc:* Harry Behn, Agnes Christine Johnston (novel by Lawrence Rising). *Ph:* John Arnold. *Art dir:* Cedric Gibbons. *Asst. dir:* David Howard. *With* Eleanor Boardman (*Fernanda*), Pat O'Malley (*Pat O'Malley*), Harrison Ford (*Don Jaime*), Trixie Friganza (*Mrs. McKee*), William J. Kelly, Rosita Marstini, George Nichols, Sojin, Evelyn Sherman, Margaret Seddon, Lillian Elliott, Priscilla Bonner. *Prod:* Metro-Goldwyn. 7 reels.

THE BIG PARADE (1926). Spectacular drama of the First World War combined with the personal story of a young soldier, his friends and family and the French girl he loves. *Sc:* Harry Behn (story by Laurence Stallings). *Ph:* John Arnold. *Titles:* Joe Farnham. *Art dir:* Cedric Gibbons, James Basevi. *Ed:* Hugh

THE BIG PARADE

Wynn. *Mus:* William Axt, David Mendoza. *With* John Gilbert (*James Apperson*), Renée Adorée (*Melisande*), Hobart Bosworth (*Mr. Apperson*), Claire McDowell (*Mrs. Apperson*), Claire Adams (*Justyn Reed*), Karl Dane (*Slim*), Robert Ober (*Harry*), Tom O'Brien, Rosita Marstini. *Prod:* King Vidor for M-G-M.

LA BOHEME (1926). The lives of friends and lovers in the Latin Quarter of Paris. *Sc:* Ray Doyle, Harry Behn (adaptation by Fred De Grasse of novel "Scenes de la vie de Bohème" by Henri Murger). *Ph:* Hendrik Sartov. *Titles:* William Conselman, Ruth Cummings. *Art dir:* Cedric Gibbons, Arnold Gillespie. *Ed:* Hugh Wynn. *Mus:* David Axt. *With*

Lillian Gish (*Mimi*), John Gilbert (*Rodolphe*), Renée Adorée (*Musette*), Roy D'Arcy (*Vicomte Paul*), George Hassell (*Schaunard*), Edward Everett Horton (*Colline*), Karl Dane (*Benoit*), Mathilde Comont (*Madame Benoit*), Gino Corrado (*Marcel*), Gene Pouyet, David Mir, Frank Currier, Catherine Vidor, Valentina Zimina, Blanche Payson. *Prod:* King Vidor for M-G-M. 9 reels. Also 1915 version made in U.S.A., and 1935 version *Mimi* (Paul Stein, G.B.).

BARDLEYS THE MAGNIFICENT (1926). Costume drama involving mistaken identity, duelling, and, of course, romance. *Sc:* Dorothy Farnum (novel by Rafael Sabatini). *Ph:* William Daniels. *Art dir:* Cedric Gibbons, James Basevi,

Richard Day. *With* John Gilbert (*Bardelys*), Eleanor Boardman (*Roxalanne de Lavedan*), Roy D'Arcy (*Chatellerault*), Lionel Belmore (*Vicomte de Lavedan*), Emily Fitzroy (*Vicomtesse de Lavedan*), George K. Arthur (*St. Eustache*), Arthur Lubin (*King Louis XIII*), Theodore von Eltz, Karl Dane, Edward Connelly, Fred Malatesta, John T. Murray, Joseph Marba, Daniel B. Tomlinson, Emile Chautard, Max Barwyn. *Prod:* M-G-M. 9 reels.

THE CROWD (1928). Story of a young married couple, representative of many others. *Sc:* King Vidor, John V. A. Weaver, Harry Behn (a story by King Vidor). *Ph:* Henry Sharp. *Titles:* Joe Farnham. *Art dir:* Cedric Gibbons, Arnold Gillespie. *Ed:* Hugh Wynn. *With* Eleanor Boardman (*Mary Sims*), James Murray (*John Sims*), Bert Roach (*Bert*), Estelle Clarke (*Jane*), Daniel G. Tomlinson (*Jim*), Freddie Burke Frederick (*Junior*), Dell Henderson, Lucy Beaumont, Alice Mildred Puter. *Prod:* M-G-M. 9 reels.

THE PATSY (G.B.: THE POLITIC FLAPPER) (1928). Comedy of a downtrodden girl who eventually has her day. *Sc:* Agnes Christine Johnston (play by Barry Connors). *Ph:* John Seitz. *Titles:* Ralph Spence. *Art dir:* Cedric Gibbons. *Ed:* Hugh Wynn. *With* Marion Davies (*Patricia Harrington*), Orville Caldwell (*Tony Anderson*), Marie Dressler (*Ma Harrington*), Dell Henderson (*Pa Harrington*), Lawrence Gray (*Billy*), Jane Winton (*Grace*). *Prod:* M-G-M. 8 reels.

SHOW PEOPLE (1928). Comedy, set in Hollywood, of a girl ambitious to be a star in the movies. *Sc:* Agnes Christine Johnson, Laurence Stallings. *Cont:* Wanda Tuchock. *Ph:* John Arnold. *Titles:*

Ralph Spence. *Art dir:* Cedric Gibbons. *Ed:* Hugh Wynn. *Mus:* (in sound version) William Axt, David Mendoza. *With* Marion Davies (*Peggy Pepper*), William Haines (*Billy Boone*), Dell Henderson (*Colonel Pepper*), Paul Ralli (*Andre*), Polly Moran (*Maid*), Albert Conti (*Producer*), Tenen Holtz, Harry Gribbon, Sidney Bracy, John Gilbert, Mae Murray, Charles Chaplin, Douglas Fairbanks, Elinor Glyn (*Themselves*), Renée Adorée, George K. Arthur, Karl Dane, Marion Davies, William S. Hart, Leatrice Joy, Rod la Roque, Louella Parsons, Aileen Pringle, Dorothy Sebastian, Norma Talmadge, Estelle Taylor, Claire Windsor (*Themselves*). *Prod:* M-G-M. 9 reels.

HALLELUJAH (1929). Drama, with all-black cast, of jealousy and murder but also noted for quieter moments. *Sc:* Wanda Tuchock (treatment by Richard Schayer from story by King Vidor). *Dial:* Ransom Rideout. *Ph:* Gordon Avil. *Titles:* Marion Ainslee. *Art dir:* Cedric Gibbons. *Ed:* Hugh Wynn, Anson Stevenson. *Mus:* traditional airs and two songs by Irving Berlin. *Asst. dir:* Robert A. Golden. *With* Daniel L. Haynes (*Zeke*), Nina Mae McKinney (*Chick*), William E. Fountaine (*Hot Shot*), Harry Gray (*Parson*), Fannie Belle De Night (*Mammy*), Everett McGarrity, Victoria Spivey, Dixie Jubilee Singers, Milton Dickerson, Robert Couch, Walter Tait. *Prod:* M-G-M. 12 reels. Also shorter silent version.

NOT SO DUMB (1930). Comedy of a madcap girl mixing in the business world. *Sc:* Wanda Tuchock (play "Dulcy" by George S. Kaufman, Marc Connelly). *Dial:* Edwin Justus Mayer. *Ph:* Oliver Marsh. *Titles:* Lucille Newmark. *Ph:*

Oliver Marsh. *Art dir:* Cedric Gibbons. *Ed:* Blanche Sewell. *Gowns:* Adrian. *Rec. Eng:* Paul Neal, Douglas Shearer. With Marion Davies (*Dulcy*), Elliott Nugent (*Gordon*), Raymond Hackett (*Bill*), Franklin Pangborn (*Leach*), Julia Faye (*Mrs. Forbes*), William Holden, Donald Ogden Stewart, Sally Starr, George Davis, Ruby Lafayette. *Prod:* M-G-M. 9 reels. Also shorter silent version. Previous version 1923 as *DULCY* (dir: Sidney A. Franklin). Re-made 1940 also as DULCY (dir: S. Sylvan Simon).

BILLY THE KID (1930). Western adventure based on the life of outlaw William Bonney. *Sc:* Wanda Tuchock (book "The Saga of Billy the Kid" by Walter Noble Burns). *Dial:* Laurence Stallings. *Add. dial:* Charles MacArthur. *Ph:* Gordon Avil. *Art dir:* Cedric Gibbons. *Ed:* Hugh Wynn. *Rec. Eng:* Paul Neal, Douglas Shearer. With John Mack Brown (*Billy*), Wallace Beery (*Garrett*), Kay Johnson (*Claire*), Wyndham Standing (*Tunston*), Karl Dane (*Swenson*), Russell Simpson (*McSween*), Blanche Frederici (*Mrs. McSween*), Roscoe Ates (*Old Stuff*), Warner P. Richmond, James Marcus, Nelson McDowell, Jack Carlyle, John Beck, Christopher Martin, Marguerita Padula, Aggie Herring. *Prod:* M-G-M. 11 reels. Roadshown in 70 mm. "Realife Grandeur" process. Re-made 1941 (David Miller, U.S.A.). Related films include *The Outlaw* (1943-50, Howard Hughes etc.). *The Kid From Texas* (G.B.: *Texas Kid—Outlaw*) (1950, Kurt Neumann); *The Left Handed Gun* (1957, Arthur Penn); *Pat Garrett and Billy The Kid* (1973, Sam Peckinpah).

STREET SCENE (1931). Realistic drama of dwellers in the tenements of New York City. *Sc:* Elmer Rice (his play). *Ph:* George Barnes. *Art dir:* Richard Day. *Ed:* Hugh Bennett. *Mus:* Alfred Newman. With Sylvia Sidney (*Rose*), William Collier Jr. (*Sam*), Estelle Taylor (*Mrs. Maurrant*), Max Montor (*Abe Kaplan*), David Landau (*Maurrant*), Russell Hopton (*Sankey*), Louis Natheaux (*Easter*), Beulah Bondi, Adele Watson, John Qualen, Harry Wallace, Greta Granstedt, T. H. Manning, Matthew McHugh, Anna Konstant, Nora Cecil, Lambert Rogers, Allan Fox, George Humbert, Eleanor Wesselhoeft, Virginia Davis, Kenneth Seiling, Helen Lovett, Conway Washburne, Howard Russell, Richard Powell, Walter James. *Prod:* Samuel Goldwyn for Goldwyn/United Artists. 80m.

THE CHAMP (1931). An old prizefighter wins the love of a child. *Sc:* Leonard Praskins (story by Frances Marion). *Dial:* Wanda Tuchock. *Ph:* Gordon Avil. *Art dir:* Cedric Gibbons. *Ed:* Hugh Wynn. *Rec Eng:* Douglas Shearer. *Asst. dir:* Robert A. Golden. With Wallace Beery (*Champ*), Jackie Cooper (*Dink*), Irene Rich (*Linda*), Roscoe Ates (*Sponge*), Edward Brophy (*Tim*), Hale Hamilton (*Tony*), Jesse Scott, Marcia Mae Jones. *Prod:* King Vidor for M-G-M. 86m. Re-made 1953 as *The Clown* (dir: Robert Z. Leonard).

BIRD OF PARADISE (1932). South Seas romance of American adventurer and native girl. *Sc:* Wells Root (adaptation by Wanda Tuchock, Leonard Praskins of play by Richard Walton Tully). *Dial:* Wells Root, Richard Walton Tully. *Ph:* Clyde de Vinna. *Mus:* Max Steiner. *Dance dir:* Busby Berkeley. With Dolores Del Rio (*Luana*), Joel McCrea (*Johnny*

Baker), John Halliday (*Mac*), Creighton Chaney (*Thornton*), Richard Gallagher (*Chester*), Pakui (*The King*), Bert Roach, Agostino Borgato, Sophie Ortego, Wade Boteler. *Prod:* David O. Selznick for RKO Radio. 80m. Re-made 1951 (dir: Delmer Daves).

CYNARA (1932). Romantic triangle drama involving rich couple and poor girl. *Sc:* Frances Marion, Lynn Starling (play by H. M. Harwood, Robert Gore-Brown, deriving from novel "An Imperfect Lover" by Robert Gore-Brown). *Ph:* Ray June. *Art dir:* Richard Day. *Ed:* Hugh Bennett. *Mus:* Alfred Newman. *With* Ronald Colman (*Jim Warlock*), Kay Francis (*Clemency*), Phyllis Barry (*Doris Lea*), Henry Stephenson (*John Tring*), Viva Tattersall (*Milly Miles*), Florine McKinney, Clarissa Selwyn, Paul Porcasi, George Kirby, Donald Stewart, Wilson Benge. *Prod:* Samuel Goldwyn for Goldwyn United Artists. 78m.

THE STRANGER'S RETURN (1933). Rural American story: the head of an Iowa family has problems. *Sc:* Brown Holmes, Phil Stong (novel by Phil Stong). *Ph:* William Daniels. *Art dir:* Frederic Hope. *Ed:* Dick Fantl. *With* Lionel Barrymore (*Grandpa Storr*), Miriam Hopkins (*Louise Storr*), Franchot Tone (*Guy Crane*), Stuart Erwin (*Simon*), Irene Hervey (*Nettie*), Beulah Bondi (*Beatrice*), Grant Mitchell, Tad Alexander, Aileen Carlyle. *Prod:* King Vidor for M-G-M. 88m.

OUR DAILY BREAD (1934). Story of unemployed men and women fighting the U. S. Depression by collective farming. *Sc:* Elizabeth Hill, King Vidor, Joseph L. Mankiewicz. *Ph:* Robert Planck. *Ed:* Lloyd Nossler. *Mus:* Alfred Newman.

Ralph Bellamy, Anna Sten and Gary Cooper in THE WEDDING NIGHT

With Karen Morley (*Mary Sims*), Tom Keene (*John Sims*), John Qualen (*Chris*), Barbara Pepper (*Sally*), Addison Richards (*Louie*), Harry Holman, Bill Engel, Frank Minor, Henry Hall, Ray Spiker, Lynton Brant, Alex Schumberg, Bud Ray, Harry Samuels. *Prod:* King Vidor for Viking Productions/United Artists. 74m.

THE WEDDING NIGHT (1935). Misleadingly titled story of famous author "away from it all" in rural Connecticut.

Sc: Edith Fitzgerald (a story by Edwin H. Knopf). *Ph:* Gregg Toland. *Art dir:* Richard Day. *Ed:* Stuart Heisler. *Cost:* Omar Kiam. *Mus:* Alfred Newman. *With* Gary Cooper (*Tony Barrett*), Anna Sten (*Manya*), Ralph Bellamy (*Fredrik*), Helen Vinson (*Dora Barrett*), Siegfried Rumann (*Nowak*), Esther Dale, Leonid Snegoff, Milla Davenport, Eleanor Wesselhoeft, Agnes Anderson, Hilda Vaughn, Walter Brennan, Douglas Wood, George Meeker, Hedi Shope, Otto Yamaoka, Violet Axelle, Ed Ebele, Robert Louis Stevenson 2nd, Auguste Tollaire, Dave Wengren, George Magrille, Bernard Siegel, Harry Semels, Robert Bolder, Alphonse Mantell, Miami Alvarez, Constance Howard, Jay Eaton, Jay Belasco, Richard Powell. *Prod:* Samuel Goldwyn for Goldwyn/United Artists. 84m.

SO RED THE ROSE (1935). Civil War romance, in many ways anticipating *Gone with the Wind. Sc:* Laurence Stallings, Maxwell Anderson, Edwin Justus Mayer (novel by Stark Young). *Ph:* Victor Milner. *Art dir:* Hans Dreier. *Ed:* Eda Warren. *Mus:* Frank Harling. *With* Margaret Sullavan (*Vallette Bedford*), Walter Connolly (*Malcolm Bedford*), Randolph Scott (*Duncan Bedford*), Janet Beecher (*Sally Bedford*), Elizabeth Patterson (*Mary Cherry*), Dickie Moore, Harry Ellerbe, Robert Cummings, Charles Starrett, Johnny Downs, Daniel Haynes, Clarence Muse, James Burke, Warner Richmond, Alfred Delcambre. *Prod:* Douglas MacLean for Paramount. 82m.

THE TEXAS RANGERS (1936). Adventure drama; three comrades split up, two to become rangers, one an outlaw. *Sc:* Louis Stevens (a story by King Vidor, Elizabeth Hill, deriving material from book by Walter Prescott Webb). *Ph:* Edward Cronjager. *Art dir:* Hans Dreier, Bernard Herzbrun. *Mus:* Sam Coslow. *With* Fred MacMurray (*Jim Hawkins*), Jack Oakie (*Wahoo*), Jean Parker (*Amanda*), Lloyd Nolan (*Sam McGee*), Edward Ellis (*Major Bailey*), Bennie Bartlett, Elena Martinez, Frank Shannon. *Prod:* King Vidor for Paramount. 95m. Re-made 1949 as *Streets of Laredo* (dir. Leslie Fenton).

STELLA DALLAS (1937). Second film of popularly soulful novel of mother love and sacrifice. *Sc:* Victor Heerman, Sarah Y. Mason (adaptation by Harry Wagstaff Gribble, Gertrude Purcell of novel by Olive Higgins Prouty). *Ph:* Rudolph Mate. *Art dir:* Richard Day. *Asst. dir:* Walter Mayo. *Cost:* Omar Kiam. *Ed:* Sherman Todd. *Mus:* Alfred Newman. *With* Barbara Stanwyck (*Stella Dallas*), John Boles (*Stephen Dallas*), Anne Shirley (*Laurel*), Barbara O'Neil (*Helen Morrison*), Alan Hale (*Ed Munn*), Marjorie Main, Edmund Elton, George Walcott, Tim Holt, Gertrude Short, Nella Walker, Bruce Satterlee, Jack Egger, Jimmy Butler, Dickie Jones, Anne Shoemaker, Al Shean. *Prod:* Samuel Goldwyn, Merritt Hulburd for Goldwyn/United Artists. 111m. Previous version 1925 (dir: Henry King).

THE CITADEL (1938). Idealistic story of young doctor and his triumph over ignorance and temptation. *Sc:* Ian Dalrymple, Frank Wead, Elizabeth Hill, Emlyn Williams (novel by A. J. Cronin). *Ph:* Harry Stradling. *Art dir:* Lazare Meerson. *Asst. dir:* Penn Tennyson. *Ed:* Charles Frend. *Mus:* Louis Levy. *With* Robert Donat (*Andrew Manson*), Rosalind Russell (*Christine*), Ralph Richard-

Robert Donat's Dr. Manson and miners in THE CITADEL

son (*Denny*), Rex Harrison (*Dr. Law-ford*), Emlyn Williams (*Owen*), Penel-ope Dudley Ward (*Toppy Leroy*), Francis L. Sullivan, Mary Clare, Cecil Parker, Nora Swinburne, Edward Chapman, Dilys Davis, Athene Seyler, Felix Aylmer, Percy Parsons, Basil Gill, Joyce Bland, P. K. Reeves, Joss Ambler. *Prod:* Victor Saville for M-G-M. British 110m.
NORTHWEST PASSAGE (BOOK ONE ROGERS' RANGERS) (1940). Spectacular adventure of Indian fighters on a long cross-country trek. *Sc:* Laurence Stallings, Talbot Jennings (novel by Kenneth Roberts). *Ph:* Sidney Wagner, William V. Skall. *Art dir:* Cedric Gibbons, Malcolm Brown. *Ed:* Conrad A. Nervig.

Mus: Herbert Stothart. *With* Spencer Tracy (*Major Robert Rogers*), Robert Young (*Langdon Towne*), Walter Brennan (*Hunk Marriner*), Ruth Hussey (*Elisabeth Browne*), Nat Pendleton (*Cap Huff*), Louis Hector, Robert Barrat, Lumsden Hare, Isabel Jewell, Douglas Walton, Addison Richards, Hugh Sothern, Montagu Love, Donald McBride, Regis Toomey, Lester Matthews, Truman Bradley. *Prod:* Hunt Stromberg for M-G-M. 125m. Technicolor.
COMRADE X (1940). Comedy romance between American in Russia and lady streetcar conductor. *Sc:* Ben Hecht, Charles Lederer (a story by Walter Reisch). *Ph:* Joseph Ruttenberg. *Art dir:*

49

Cedric Gibbons. *Ed:* Harold F. Kress. *Mus:* Bronislau Kaper. *With* Clark Gable (*McKinley B. Thomson*), Hedy Lamarr (*Theodora*), Oscar Homolka (*Vasiliev*), Felix Bressart (*Vanya*), Eve Arden (*Jane Wilson*), Sig Rumann (*Emil Von Hofer*), Natasha Lytess (*Olga*), Vladimir Sokoloff, John Piccori, Edgar Barrier, Mikhail Rasumny. *Prod:* Gottfried Reinhardt for M-G-M. 90m.

H. M. PULHAM, ESQ. (1941). Social comedy of refined young Bostonian in New York on a spree. *Sc:* Elizabeth Hill, King Vidor (the novel by John P. Marquand). *Ph:* Ray June. *Art dir:* Cedric Gibbons. *Ed:* Harold F. Kress. *Mus:* Bronislau Kaper. *With* Robert Young (*Harry Pulham*), Hedy Lamarr (*Marvin Myles*), Ruth Hussey (*Kay Motford*), Charles Coburn (*Mr. Pulham Sr.*), Van Heflin (*Bill King*), Fay Holden (*Mrs. Pulham*), Bonita Granville, Douglas Wood, Charles Halton. Leif Erickson, Phil Brown, David Clyde, Sara Haden. *Prod:* King Vidor for M-G-M. 120m.

AN AMERICAN ROMANCE (1944). Ambitious study in American life centered on the success story of a poor immigrant. *Sc:* Herbert Dalmas, William Ludwig (a story by King Vidor). *Ph:* Harold Rosson. *Art dir:* Cedric Gibbons, Urie McCleary. *Ed:* Conrad A. Nervig. *Mus:* Louis Gruenberg. *With* Brian Donlevy (*Steve Dangos*), Ann Richards

Vidor and Hedy Lamarr on H. M. PULHAM, ESQ.

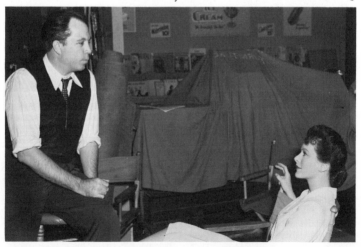

(*Anna*), Walter Abel (*Howard Clinton*), John Qualen (*Anton Dubechek*), Horace McNally (*Teddy Dangos*), Robert Lowell, Mary McLeod, Ray Teal, Jackie 'Butch' Jenkins. *Prod:* King Vidor for M-G-M. 151m. Technicolor.

DUEL IN THE SUN (1947). Elaborate Western adventure and erotic romance. *Sc:* David O. Selznick (novel by Niven Busch, adapted by Oliver H. P. Garrett). *Ph:* Lee Garmes, Harold Rosson, Ray Rennahan. *Art dir:* James Basevi, John Ewing. *Ed:* Hal C. Kern, William Ziegler, John Faure. *Mus:* Dimitri Tiomkin. *With* Jennifer Jones (*Pearl Chavez*), Joseph Cotten (*Jesse McCanles*), Gregory Peck (*Lewt McCanles*), Lionel Barrymore (*Senator McCanles*), Lillian Gish (*Laura Belle McCanles*), Walter Huston (*The Sinkiller*), Herbert Marshall (*Scott Chavez*), Charles Bickford, Joan Tetzel, Harry Carey, Otto Kruger, Sidney Blackmer, Tilly Losch, Scott McKay, Butterfly McQueen, Francis McDonald, Victor Kilian, Griff Barnett, Steve Dunhill, Lane Chandler, Lloyd Shaw, Thomas Dillon. Narration by Orson Welles. Additional uncredited direction by William Dieterle, Josef von Sternberg, William Cameron Menzies and others. *Prod:* David O. Selznick for Vanguard Productions/Selznick Releasing Organization. 138m. Technicolor.

A MIRACLE CAN HAPPEN (1948). Portmanteau film with separate vignettes connected by a reporter's inquiry. *Co-dir:* Leslie Fenton. *Sc:* Laurence Stallings, Lou Breslow, John O'Hara (a story by Arch Oboler). *Ph:* John F. Seitz, Edward Cronjager, Joseph Biroc, Gordon Avil. *Art dir:* Ernest Fegté, Duncan Cramer. *Ed:* James Smith. *Mus:* Heinz Roemheld, David Chudnow, Skitch Henderson. *With* Burgess Meredith (*Oliver Pease*), Paulette Goddard (*Martha Pease*), James Stewart (*Slim*), Henry Fonda (*Lank*), Dorothy Lamour (*Gloria Manners*), Victor Moore (*Ashton Carrington*), Fred MacMurray (*Al*), Hugh Herbert, Harry James, William Demarest, Dorothy Ford, Eduardo Ciannelli, David Whorf, Eileen Janssen, Charles D. Brown, Betty Caldwell, Frank Moran, Tom Fadden, Paul Hurst. *Prod:* Benedict Bogeaus, Burgess Meredith for Miracle Productions/United Artists. 107m. Uncredited direction of Fonda-Stewart sequence by George Stevens and John Huston. Retitled *On Our Merry Way* soon after release.

THE FOUNTAINHEAD (1949). Romantic drama arguing the rights of personal freedom. *Sc:* Ayn Rand (her novel). *Ph:* Robert Burks. *Art dir:* Edward Carrere. *Asst. dir:* Dick Mayberry. *Ed:* David Weisbart. *Mus:* Max Steiner. *With* Gary Cooper (*Howard Roark*), Patricia Neal (*Dominique*), Raymond Massey (*Gail Wynand*), Kent Smith (*Peter Keating*), Robert Douglas (*Ellsworth Toohey*), Henry Hull (*Henry Cameron*), Ray Collins (*Enright*), Moroni Olsen, Jerome Cowan, Paul Harvey, Harry Woods, Paul Stanton, Bob Alden, Tristram Coffin, Roy Gordon, Isabel Withers, Almira Sessions, Tito Vuolo, William Haade, Gail Bonney, Thurston Hall, Dorothy Christy, Harlan Warde, Jonathan Hale, Frank Wilcox, Douglas Kennedy, Pierre Watkin, Selmar Jackson, John Doucette, John Alvin, Geraldine Wall, Fred Kelsey, Paul Newland, George Sherwood, Lois Austin, Josephine Whittell, Lester Dorr, Bill Dagwell, Charles Trowbridge, Russell Hicks, Raymond Largay, Charles Evans, Morris

Ankrum, Griff Barnett, G. Pat Collins, Ann Doran, Ruthelma Stevens, Creighton Hale, Philo McCullough. *Prod:* Henry Blanke for Warner Bros. 114m.

BEYOND THE FOREST (1949). Story of a Midwestern "Madame Bovary," more aggressive than her model. *Sc:* Lenore Coffee (novel by Stuart Engstrand). *Ph:* Robert Burks. *Art dir:* Robert Haas. *Ed:* Rudi Fehr. *Mus:* Max Steiner. *With* Bette Davis (*Rosa Moline*), Joseph Cotten (*Dr. Lewis Moline*), David Brian (*Neil Latimer*), Ruth Roman (*Carol*), Minor Watson (*Moose*), Dona Drake, Regis Toomey, Sarah Selby, Mary Servoss, Frances Charles, Creighton Hale, Harry Tyler, Robert Littlefield, Joel Allen, Ann Doran. *Prod:* Henry Blanke for Warner Bros. 97m.

LIGHTNING STRIKES TWICE (1951). Brooding drama of murder and frustration in atmospheric desert locale. *Sc:* Lenore Coffee (novel "A Man without Friends" by Margaret Echard). *Ph:* Sid Hickox. *Art dir:* Douglas Bacon. *Ed:* Thomas Reilly. *Mus:* Max Steiner. *With* Richard Todd (*Richard Trevelyan*), Ruth Roman (*Shelley Carnes*), Zachary Scott (*Harvey Turner*), Mercedes McCambridge (*Liza McStringer*), Frank Conroy (*J. D. Nolan*), Kathryn Givney (*Myrna Nolan*), Darryl Hickman, Rhys Williams, Nacho Galindo. *Prod:* Henry Blanke for Warner Bros. 91m.

JAPANESE WAR BRIDE (1952). Story of young American and his Oriental bride overcoming racial misunderstandings. *Sc:* Catherine Turney (a story by Anson Bond). *Ph:* Lionel Lindon. *Art dir:* Danny Hall. *Asst. dir:* Wilbur McGaugh. *Ed:* Terry Morse. *Mus:* Emil Newman, Arthur Lange. *With* Shirley Yamaguchi

Richard Todd and Ruth Roman in
LIGHTNING STRIKES TWICE

(*Tae Shimizu*), Don Taylor (*Jim Sterling*), Cameron Mitchell (*Art Sterling*), Marie Windsor (*Fran Sterling*), James Bell (*Ed Sterling*), Louise Lorimer (*Harriet Sterling*), Philip Ahn, Sybil Merritt, Lane Nakano, Kathleen Mulqueen, Orley Lindgren, George Wallace, May Takasugi, William Yokota, Susie Matsumoto, Weaver Levy, Jerry Fujikawa, Chieko Sato, Tetsu Komai, Hisa Chiba, David March. *Prod:* Joseph Bernhard, Anson Bond for Bernhard Productions/20th Century-Fox. 91m.

RUBY GENTRY (1952). A passionate girl crosses over from the "wrong side of the tracks." *Sc:* Sylvia Richards (a story by Arthur Fitz-Richard). *Ph:* Russell Harlan. *Art dir:* Danny Hall. *Asst. dir:* Milton Carter. *Ed:* Terry Morse. *Mus:* Heinz Roemheld, David Chudnow. *With* Jennifer Jones (*Ruby Gentry*), Charlton Heston (*Boake Tackman*), Karl Malden (*Jim Gentry*), Tom Tully (*Jud Corey*), Bernard Phillips (*Dr. Manfred*), James Anderson (*Jewell Corey*), Josephine Hutchinson, Phyllis Avery, Herbert Heyes, Myra Marsh, Charles Cane, Sam Flint, Frank Wilcox. *Prod:* Joseph Bernhard, King Vidor for Bernhard-Vidor Productions/20th Century-Fox. 82m.

MAN WITHOUT A STAR (1955). Sturdy ranching western, with more than usual humour and authentic detail. *Sc:* Borden Chase, D. D. Beauchamp (novel by Dee Linford). *Ph:* Russell Metty. *Art dir:* Alexander Golitzen, Richard H. Riedel. *Asst. dir:* Frank Shaw. *Ed:* Virgil Vogel. *Mus:* Joseph Gershenson. *With* Kirk Douglas (*Dempsey Rae*), Jeanne Crain (*Reed Bowman*), Claire Trevor (*Idonee*), William Campbell (*Jeff Jimson*), Jay C. Flippen (*Strap Davis*), Richard Boone (*Steve Miles*), Myrna Hansen, Mara Corday, Eddy C. Waller, Frank Chase, Sheb Wooley, George Wallace, Paul Birch, Roy Barcroft, William "Bill" Phillips, Millicent Patrick, Casey MacGregor, Jack Ingram, Ewing Mitchell, William Challee, James Hayward. *Prod:* Aaron Rosenberg for Universal-International. 89m. Technicolor. Re-made 1968 as *A Man Called Gannon* (dir: James Goldstone).

WAR AND PEACE or GUERRA E PACE (1956). Large-scale filming of

WAR AND PEACE: top, Herbert Lom as Napoleon. Below, Mel Ferrer and Audrey Hepburn

53

Gina Lollobrigida in
SOLOMON AND SHEBA

classic novel. *Sc:* Bridget Boland, Robert Westerby, King Vidor, Mario Camerini, Ennio De Concini, Ivo Perilli (novel by Leo Tolstoy). *Ph:* Jack Cardiff, Aldo Tonti. *Art dir:* Mario Chiari. *Ed:* Stuart Gilmore, Leo Catosso. *Mus:* Nino Rota. *With* Audrey Hepburn (*Natasha*), Henry Fonda (*Pierre*), Mel Ferrer (*Andrey*), Vittorio Gassman (*Anatole*), Anita Ekberg (*Helene*), Oscar Homolka (*General Kutuzov*), Herbert Lom (*Napoleon*), John Mills, Helmut Dantine, Milly Vitale, Barry Jones, Lea Seidl, Wilfred Lawson, Tullio Carminati, Jeremy Brett, Sean Barrett, Anna Maria Ferrero, May Britt, Patrick Crean, Gertrude Flynn. *Prod:* Carlo Ponti, Dino De Laurentiis for Ponti-De Laurentiis/Paramount. 208m. Technicolor. VistaVision. Acknowledged additional direction by Mario Soldati.

Previous Russian version 1915 (dir: Yakov Protazanov, Pyotr Chardynin); U.S.S.R. version 1965 (dir: Sergei Bondarchuk).

SOLOMON AND SHEBA (1959). Biblical spectacular culled from the Old Testament. *Sc:* Anthony Veiller, Paul Dudley, George Bruce (a story by Crane Wilbur). *Ph:* Freddie Young. *Art dir:* Richard Day, Alfred Sweeney. *Ed:* John Ludwig. *Mus:* Mario Nascimbene. *With* Yul Brynner (*Solomon*), Gina Lollobrigida (*Sheba*), George Sanders (*Adonijah*), David Farrar (*Pharoah*), Marisa Pavan (*Abishag*), John Crawford (*Joab*), Laurence Naismith, Jose Nieto, Alejandro Rey, Harry Andrews, Julio Pena, Finlay Currie, William Devlin, Jean Anderson, Jack Gwillim. *Prod:* Edward Small, Ted Richmond for Theme Pictures/United Artists. 139m. Technicolor. Super Technirama 70mm.

King Vidor's contribution to *The Wizard of Oz* (1939) is noted in the essay. According to Mr. Vidor, the final scene of *Northwest Passage* was directed by Jack Conway. In 1954 Vidor directed some sequences for *Light's Diamond Jubilee,* a television spectacular, produced by David O. Selznick. Since his most recent feature, *Solomon and Sheba,* he has made a 16mm. short film entitled *Truth and Illusion: An Introduction to Metaphysics.*

Additional material for this filmography researched and prepared by Jean and Kingsley Canham.

King Vidor directing SOLOMON AND SHEBA

JOHN CROMWELL: Memories of Love, Elegance and Style

"Handling women was governed mostly by the nature of the parts. I never made any point, as Cukor has at times, of developing their feminine aspects; I was always guided by the nature of the part so I was never conscious of developing skills or handling personalities."

[Interview with Cromwell, January 10, 1974]

"Women's pictures" have become a part of Hollywood history, and are generally associated with three major sources: directors, studios and stars. At the height of their careers, Bette Davis, Barbara Stanwyck, Joan Crawford and Katharine Hepburn were able to dictate terms to their studios which had a direct bearing on the quality and the nature of the roles that they played. Bette Davis fought an unsuccessful case against Warner Brothers in the mid Thirties; her contemporary, Olivia de Havilland, won a similar case some years later. Thus, in many instances, they had the right not only to refuse roles that they considered unsuitable, but they could also choose the director and approve the script before shooting commenced.

I have not included script-writers as one of the major sources, partly because of the vast range of material encompassed by this sort of film, and partly because the script credits are frequently misleading or inaccurate in that they do not specify the precise nature of the collaboration or always identify all the writers involved. Enough has been written elsewhere about the differing background "look" with which each studio earmarked its product, and the proliferation of old films on television and at repertory cinemas should provide the average viewer with ample evidence to substantiate the various claims, and to accept that these have a

Portrait of John Cromwell by Maurice Goldberg

particular relevance to the "woman's picture." D. W. Griffith was the first American director to emphasise the role of women in his films; amongst others to follow his example were John Stahl, Douglas Sirk, Frank Borzage (undoubtedly the cinema's most *romantic* director), Vincente Minnelli and John Cromwell, as well as the most famous of all, George Cukor.

They are mostly immediately linked with particular actresses: e.g. Griffith with Lillian Gish; Minnelli with Judy Garland; Cukor with Katharine Hepburn; or Sirk with Lauren Bacall and Dorothy Malone. But few have worked with such a wide range, and have been as consistently successful in obtaining such a high quality of distaff performances as John Cromwell whose films have starred Nancy Carroll, Madeleine Carroll, Mary Astor, Irene Dunne, Bette Davis, Betty Field, Frances Dee, Katharine Hepburn, Ann Harding, Kay Francis, Hedy Lamarr, Carole Lombard and Lizabeth Scott among others. Nor did he work with a major studio when he made his name; he started with Paramount during their financial doldrums, and transferred to R.K.O. where his association with David O. Selznick led him into the bigger leagues, enabling him to give greater scope to the style and sheer professionalism of his work. Possibly his rapport with players came from his stage experience; certainly it was as an actor that Paramount put him under contract in October, 1928. Soon after his screen *début* in *The Dummy* (1929), he was given the chance to direct *Close Harmony* and *The Dance of Life* in collaboration with Edward Sutherland, and he remained behind the cameras for most of his film career.

•   •   •

He saw his collaboration with Sutherland as a two-way education, but the studio undoubtedly saw it as a safety measure. In the panic which ensued with the changeover to sound, studios

John Cromwell with Ruth Chattertón
in his screen debut, THE DUMMY

hired stage directors because of their presumed knowledge of the
best manner for handling dialogue; this step returned the director to the prominence that the position had held in the early days
of the cinema, but it held its own problems as the studios discovered when many new directors turned out static stage material
which soon soured audiences. Thus Paramount's scheme of teaming a new director with an experienced professional was a form
of insurance policy.

Fortunately, the nature of the collaboration was a happy one
since they were soon faced with a more serious problem. The

night before *The Dance of Life* was scheduled to begin shooting, the studio was seriously damaged by a major fire. The studio executives had no choice but to introduce a system of all night working to catch up when production was resumed; also night shooting offered a way around the makeshift sound proofing of the stage since there was a minimum of traffic noise.

Cromwell also had problems with the techniques involved in his new medium: "I never got accustomed to the terrific range of the camera, and what the choice of shot can do to a scene. I remember DeMille had a sign in his office that read 'Say it with props,' emphasising the fact that this was a visual medium. I was always very aware of composition. I had to rely enormously on my cameramen, especially at first. I was never able to learn much about lighting because it seemed to me that every cameraman I had was so different from the last one in his technique that it became almost impossible to learn unless you just took time out and devoted yourself to it. So I had to be completely at their mercy. I would talk, mostly about how I felt about a scene, what it meant to me in terms of lighting, as near as I could tell, and rely entirely upon them. But I was very lucky, I had some wonderful cameramen—wonderful in that they never let me down . . . men like Jimmy Howe, Charlie Lang, Arthur Miller." [Interview with Leonard Maltin in "Action"; May–June 1973].

He was born Elwood Dager in Toledo, Ohio, on 23rd December 1887. After he graduated in 1905 from the Howe School, in Howe, Indiana, he immediately began his stage career acting with touring and stock companies. He was billed as Elwood Dager until a New York appearance in 1912 when he changed his name to John Cromwell. In 1913 he received his first stage assignment as a director for a production of "The Painted Woman," while from 1915 to 1919 he worked as an actor and stage director for the New York Repertory Company and appeared in the American *pre-*

mières of George Bernard Shaw's "Major Barbara" (Playhouse, December 9th, 1915) and "Captain Brassbound's Conversion" (Playhouse, March 29th 1916). His career was briefly interrupted by service in the United States Army during the First World War, but after the war he soon returned to acting, as well as producing on Broadway and for various regional theatres in the United States and Britain. Although he primarily worked as a film director from 1929 to the late Fifties, he still found time to return to the Broadway stage as an actor and director.

"I signed my first contract with Paramount in the spring of 1928. David [O. Selznick] had joined Paramount not long before that as Ben Schulberg's assistant but I didn't have too much to do with him until some time later when he was preparing his first production as a producer, a picture to be called *The Street of Chance,* and David asked me to direct it. It created quite a stir throughout the industry [Note: It was a thinly veiled story about Arnold Rothstein, the gambler known as "The King of the Roaring Twenties"], and David and I found we hit it off very well together. I was always a great admirer of David. . . . There is a little bit of history connected with our meeting that I'm sure you aren't aware of. I had gone to Hollywood in the spring of '28 to play the leading role with Eddie Robinson in 'The Racket.' The play made quite a hit and I was offered my contract but I had to explain that I had signed a contract to play the leading part in a new play, 'The Gentlemen of the Press' [later filmed with Walter Huston in the leading role], due to open in New York in September. Schulberg explained that that was quite alright. They would take up the film contract after I finished the play. We opened one week after a play called 'The Front Page'! If you know your history well enough you will readily understand why we ran for only two weeks, and that by the end of the month I was on my way to Hollywood to take up my film contract! I remember remarking to myself at the time that David and Walter Wanger [for whom Cromwell made *Algiers* (1938)] were undoubtedly the only two university men in the motion picture business in an executive position."

"When I first went to Paramount, George Bancroft was their biggest star and, as George had had some stage experience, I was assigned to three of his pictures. To buy my way out of that assignment I agreed to do one more if I was given *A Farewell to Arms* with Gary [Cooper] and Helen Hayes. Then my friend Ben Schulberg was fired, and the producer of the picture got his friend, Frank Borzage, in to direct. I walked off the lot and Myron Selznick, who was my agent, put me over with David who was, by that time, in charge of R.K.O. R.K.O. was always an endearing place to me; it had a distinct feeling of independence and individuality it never lost. It was always short of good writers, good directors and good actors, but it would never admit it. At this time the business was absolutely fascinating as the industry was frantically adapting itself to sound, and every day was decorated with red letters. As I remember, I was held spellbound by a cameraman named Roy Hunt. I used him on several pictures because he was so interested in everything. He was a loquacious Southerner and as mechanically inventive as anyone I ever saw. Almost every week he would appear with a new camera cover or an ingenious camera dolly for getting through small doors, etc." [Letter to the author, dated 15th October 1973.]

At the time of writing, I have been unable to see any of the Paramount films which Cromwell directed, but I was able to talk to him about them when he visited London:

"*The Texan* was an O. Henry story, and he was still a very popular writer then; the ending had its usual O. Henry twist and it seemed a very good part for Gary Cooper. David Selznick's first picture, *The Street of Chance*, did very well and created quite a

Cromwell directs. Left, pointing at Lucien Littlefield during work on
TOM SAWYER (Jackie Coogan with pea-shooter). Right, in front of
camera watching George Bancroft and young David Durand rehearsing
for a scene in RICH MAN'S FOLLY

stir, and stirs were not too frequent in those days. Many of them
were just routine, they just turned them out. . . . *Rich Man's Folly*
was a very good opportunity; it was a modern dress version of
Dickens' 'Dombey and Son,' and it should have been absolutely
splendid for Bancroft except that it required in the actor a consciousness of the material—of which he had none! To him it was
always just another part to play in the same old manner. He had
no realisation of the opportunities that were there, so they were
simply missed.

"*The World and the Flesh* was the high point of degradation
from my point of view. It was such an asinine, concocted story!
I had personally taken a great interest in the Russian Revolution
and the way it happened, and had heard a great deal from a jour-
nalist we had at the time named Lincoln Steffens who had been
in Moscow at the time it happened. I had heard him lecture, and

had been thrilled by his recounting of the events. And so I had an idea of what chances there were to do a real picture. Then to have this . . . this almost disgusting tale, the same old hash served up as a script! I made up my mind that would be the last of it, I would try to get away.

"In the matter of rehearsals for pictures, I went through a lot of varying experiences. Firstly at Paramount, there was a great aura about the men from the New York stage and their experience with dialogue. The attitude of almost everybody in the studio at the time reflected an absolute fear . . . a panic at what was going to happen to their careers with sound coming in, so they really laid down the red carpet for me. So I always had rehearsals until it came to *For The Defense* with Bill Powell and Kay Francis, where we had a schedule of 2½ weeks. I set up the usual rehearsal schedule, but at the production meeting Schulberg said: 'We can't have any more rehearsals, John.' I asked what he meant, and he continued: 'It's a waste of time. The directors don't know what to do with rehearsals, they've not been used to them so the time is wasted.' I had noticed this, too, but had improved every minute of my time with rehearsals, so I said: 'Well, you know you don't have to do that with me, you know I don't waste any time.' 'If I give you the privilege, they'll all want it, and that will just create a situation,' said Schulberg. So I said: 'I tell you what I'll do, Ben. I'll reduce the schedule one day for every two days' rehearsal you give me.' And he replied: 'You can't do it, mechanically you can't do it. You just won't get around fast enough.' But I said: 'However, that stands.' I think I ended up with four days rehearsal, cutting two days off the shooting schedule. Incredible! I couldn't believe it years afterwards."

❉ ❉ ❉

Cromwell's move to R.K.O. resulted in a series of soap operas and films about family strife which enabled him to extend the characterisations of his players as he was able to work on the scripts. Lionel Barrymore in *Sweepings* is very restrained and in tune with the rest of the cast. *The Silver Cord*, which Cromwell had directed on the stage, contains a series of excellent performances; the dialogue is forceful, but not pedantic, and, while one is aware of the stage origin of the material, it is not distracting (like Lowell Sherman's *Morning Glory*, a contemporary R.K.O. vehicle for Hepburn) thanks to the skill and familiarity Cromwell brings to his staging—for instance, the parallel drawn between the mother's influence on her two sons and prospective daughter-in-laws. Irene Dunne realises that unless she cuts Joel McCrea adrift from his mother's apron strings their married life will be ruined, but Frances Dee is unable to stand up for herself or Eric Linden as effectively.

Cromwell himself feels that, at this stage, he had begun to get a really good idea of the form that scripts should take . . . the fact that pictures are a *graphic* art. He realised that the best writers came from the newspaper business since they were trained as reporters to come and describe what they *saw*. He personally welcomed the assignment of *The Silver Cord* because of his knowledge of the play, the writer and his intentions, and he felt he could pull it off better than any other director. He followed this with *Double Harness*, a shrewd and sophisticated interior drama about Ann Harding's efforts to get and hold on to William Powell as a husband after her machinations are revealed. *Spitfire* was quite definitely a character study rather than a narration of events, the love theme providing interest only as far as Katharine Hepburn's reactions are concerned. Her individuality was stressed by the background of the primitive mountain community viewing her as a witch/healer-cum-outcast. Cromwell does not like the film much, as he started it with the conviction that Hepburn was totally unsuited to the part:

"She was riding her bid for popularity, she tried to take complete advantage of everything she had won, but we got along very well until . . . you see, I was still finding my way with the camera and I had certainly not progressed to the point where I didn't have to worry about what I called my 'homework.' When I was arranging individual scenes, I still had to prepare it so that when I came on the set I had a definite idea of what I was going to do. Being a well disciplined person, I was very conscious of cost, and I couldn't just sit around and make up my mind whether they were going to cross over here or there while we were on the set. So I had all the business arranged, and she came to me one time and said: 'I'd like to cross this way.' I refused, explaining why in terms of character and motivation, and we had quite a situation until I told her finally that I couldn't do it. She felt pretty hurt; we eventually resolved it, but I think those things were reflected in the picture."

I agree with Cromwell's conviction that the accent which she used was unusual and not at all convincing, but I feel that she brings the character to life in spite of this impediment. The film covers much the same ground as Hathaway's *The Trail of the Lonesome Pine* (1936), even opening with a similar explanatory title about the mountain folk and their strange beliefs and customs, ending with the hope that "faith [is] simple and strong enough to turn a light on civilisation." The faith is that of Hepburn, who heals through prayer and her stolen Sunday School cards in between bouts of asserting her independence by stoning passersby for trespassing on her path, or knocking out a man with a well-aimed bolt for kissing her.

She falls for a glib engineer in spite of herself ("If I believed all the things you said, my head would be a'swimmin'"), but his solid, dependable boss is the man who protects her when she

A coy love scene between Katharine Hepburn and Robert Young
as her deceitful lover in SPITFIRE

steals a baby which she feels the parents were neglecting. But,
as I have said, the narrative is unimportant; the film is based on
a play but Cromwell opens out his material with the aid of Edward
Cronjager's mobile camera following Hepburn's movements
through soliloquies, and several titles help speed up the action.

The dewy, soft-key lighting and the composition are outstanding;
memorable shots include Hepburn seen in long shot behind a
bush, her face a white speck as she shouts to Bellamy in the foreground; an overhead shot looking down on Young and Hepburn
as they lie under a pine tree; a lateral track with the angry group
of men storming across the woods with a background of natural
sound, and a close-up of Hepburn's tear-stained face as she prays

without her cards, the camera keeping a single tear in focus as she turns her head. But, above all, one remembers Hepburn's eccentricities, the tomboyish nature and the tinny, sometimes breathless voice, and the delicate use of her hands as in the above-mentioned shot with Young where she holds his hand, gently moving her other hand across her chest and body as if spreading or absorbing the feel of his flesh as she looks into his eyes and expresses her love, finally rolling off-camera over the pine needles on which they have been lying, or the exuberant cartwheel she spins as she approaches her house, regaining her feet to burst open the door and launch a basket of laundry into the air with a flying kick. Her physical celebrations of the joys of life and love make this an eccentric and likeable film.

The Silver Cord, Of Human Bondage and *The Racket* are all about various forms of tyranny. The first was a very daring play and film in that it attacked one of the sacred cows: motherhood. The excellent playing of a small cast is dominated by Laura Hope Crews's fidgety, monstrous mother, shifting ground from direct (fraudulent) emotional and selfish appeals to bursts of outright aggression and pure outrageousness; it is a *coup de théâtre* from the moment she splits her newly-wed son and his bride into separate bedrooms; her eventual downfall when Dunne succeeds in taking McCrea from her is tempered by her retention of Linden, just as Mitchum's victory over racketeer Ryan in *The Racket* is sobered by the thought that a new day is dawning with more battles to fight. *Of Human Bondage* is only slightly more optimistic in its final moments of the story of the tart without a heart.

The title of this essay derived from my personal reaction to a number of Cromwell films viewed during its compilation. A belated viewing of *The Fountain* (1934) establishes it as a key film, embodying all of these qualities: memories of love motivating relationships between Ann Harding, Brian Aherne and Paul

Lukas in a story that is presented in a manner and with *décor* which can aptly be described as elegant, and directed with great assurance and style.

The sensitivity and low-keyed nature of the direction and the leading performances are aided by some beautifully composed soft-focus photography and a surprisingly non-verbose script, and these advantages overcome the occasional drawbacks of the over-lavish *décor* and a rather syrupy Steiner score. The film opens against a musical background, with high-key shots of a train carrying English officers to a Dutch internment camp during the First World War, notable for the scene's absence of dialogue—this type of motif is picked up again when Ann Harding plays the piano and the camera cuts away from her to record the silent reactions of members of her family or friends.

The metaphysical content of the film is stressed by a verse from Coleridge's "Dejection" that appears at the end of the credits:

> From outward forms to win
> the passion and the life
> from the fountains within.

Although this dominates the film, the method of presentation reflects Cromwell's style: the camera movements represent the restlessness and soul-searching of both Aherne and Harding; the aforementioned use of a musical track to eliminate the need for dialogue, and the build-up to the entrance of both Harding and her German husband, Paul Lukas. Under the terms of a general parole, Aherne is sent to live with Harding, an old English friend who is spending the war in neutral Holland with a titled family at her husband's insistence. Soon after he arrives, Aherne is seen at a window; glancing out, he sees his friend, Ralph Forbes, walking with Ann Harding in the garden. They are talking about

Aherne, and their voices carry into the room as he listens, smiling happily at Harding's anticipation of seeing him again. At one point, he calls to her, but she is going away from him out of ear-shot. The scene changes to a formal family grouping before sup-per, the camera pans across to the door, and focuses on Harding ascending the stairs, tracking back as she enters the room.

The family are shown as being concerned with appearances; the spinsterish daughter, Sophie (Sara Haden), cuts a grim figure in her black apparel; her vindictive outlook, anti-British feelings, and closed mind, in spite of her literary pursuits, are soon appar-ent (at a tennis match later on, the general nationalistic feelings of the family emerge as open hostility flares between Harding and them). In view of this family hostility, it comes as no sur-prise to hear Harding describe herself as "an outside breed," and her slip when she reveals to Aherne that she does not love Lukas is in keeping with the forthright nature of her character.

Since she has found refuge in her renewed friendship with Aherne, she is naturally somewhat disturbed to learn that Lukas has been invalided out of the war and is on his way to join them. Lukas is mentioned in dialogue, but our first glimpse of him is by way of a portrait; on hearing that Aherne too is returning, Sophie stands under Lukas's portrait with a look of longing (sug-gesting she may hold an impossible love for him?); later Ann Harding slumps against a bay window, clenching and unclench-ing her hands as her mother-in-law knits and Sophie reads, paus-ing to glance meaningfully at the portrait of Lukas as the sound of his car arriving is heard. Cromwell's economic use of lap dis-solves to eliminate unnecessary actions increases the atmosphere that Harding describes as "living under an enchantment or spell."

A moment of truth is at hand for Ann Harding as she is pressed by Paul Lukas as her crippled husband in THE FOUNTAIN

In spite of her delicate appearance, underlined with gestures such as her involuntary clutch at the top of her dress near the throat as she reads of Lukas's wounds, and Cromwell's *penchant* for composing shots around her with candles flickering in the foreground, Ann Harding has a winning directness in speaking her mind; Aherne and Lukas reflect gentleness, integrity and dignity; and Jean Hersholt contributes a well-rounded cameo as an understanding father, countering the malice of Sara Haden's role. *The Fountain* is undoubtedly one of Cromwell's most outstanding achievements, and remains one of his favourite films today.

* * *

One of the most interesting aspects of Cromwell's version of *Of Human Bondage* (1934) is the style with which he captures the essence of the woman's picture—emotion. And he does so without the trappings of the Bette Davis vehicles at Warners, or the plush, highly-coloured over-emotionalism of Ross Hunter's work at Universal in the Fifties and Sixties.

His film seems like a plot outline or shorthand version of one of these later examples in that it packs a concise story into eighty-three powerful minutes compared to their overblown 120-minute average. Camera set-ups are reduced to a minimum; close shots replace two shots and medium shots; tracking shots proliferate with a special emphasis on Leslie Howard's club-foot; and the key scenes suddenly explode across the screen as the camera pulls back to locate them in their context, e.g. the first shot of Mildred (Bette Davis) bursting into laughter in the restaurant as she serves Muller (Alan Hale), or a later shot of her lying, speechlessly sobbing in the gutter, as Griffiths (Reginald Denny) rejects her, having seduced her away from his friend Howard, and orders a policeman to take her away.

The camera movement seems to represent the emotional state

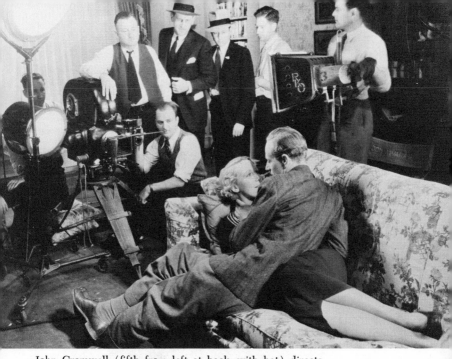

John Cromwell (fifth from left at back, with hat) directs
Leslie Howard and Kay Johnson in OF HUMAN BONDAGE

of the characters—several times the screen fades into a blur as
Howard fantasises about Mildred after she has treated him abominably (Cromwell feels this was due more to hewing to the script
than to a conscious directorial touch). There is a bare minimum
of sets, probably because of budget limitations, but this sparsity
is used to advantage by Cromwell to supplement the visual indications of the unreality of Howard's day-to-day existence. His
affair with the wealthy Nora (Kay Johnson) is doomed to failure
as she is a *fiction* writer for a woman's magazine—a further retreat
into fantasy and the trap of his obsession. Reality is difficult enough

for him to face; for instance, the scene at the Medical School where the tutor's impersonal observations about his club-foot (offering more interesting possibilities for clinical research than that of the guinea-pig patient) become offensive. The underlying implication of the sequence is that Howard is more sensitive to the remarks as a result of his obsession with Mildred, which has heightened his self-consciousness about the deformity. Again in the climax when he proposes to Sally (Frances Dee), he is obviously still mentally involved with the dead Mildred; their voices are drowned out by the noise of the traffic, and we last see two ordinary people, vanishing into a taxi with a noticeably muted enthusiasm over the prospect of their future life.

Similarly, whenever Mildred is being nice to Carey (Leslie Howard), the camera catches the nervous movement of her hands and eyes, as she circles around him and baits her trap, after mov-

Bette Davis and Leslie Howard work on a scene in OF HUMAN BONDAGE excised from the final cut

ing behind him to lie out of his line of vision, although her voice usually betrays her to the audience.

Miss Davis admirably projects the vulgarity and venality of the character without presenting a suggestion of depth—but then Mildred is a pretty shallow person. She is matched by the gentlemanly understatement of Howard's playing, yet he is sufficiently fluent an actor to prevent her dominating the film as she used to do at Warners with male leads of limited talent such as George Brent or Paul Henreid.

Later versions of *Of Human Bondage* failed through poor scripting and very indifferent acting; even the most ridiculous plot can be carried if the cast are capable—e.g. *Madame X* (1965, David Lowell Rich) with Lana Turner giving a performance of a lifetime by taking the *clichéd,* over-melodramatic material quite seriously—and directors like Cromwell and John Stahl proved this time and again with their successful series of low budget "women's pictures" which set a precedent for Douglas Sirk's work at Universal in the Fifties.

✿　✿　✿

Anthony Veiller's screenplay for *Jalna* (1935) was based on a series of novels by Mazo de la Roche, outlining the history of a Canadian family through a number of generations; the result is a hotch-potch of previously successful Cromwell "soap opera" themes involving family interference in marriage (cf. *The Silver Cord*); a married woman falling in love with another man (cf. *The Fountain*), and general familial strife (cf. *Rich Man's Folly* and *Sweepings*). The film is stagebound (again budget limitations possibly restricted the use of exteriors in any very purposeful form) and stiffly and unconvincingly acted by most of the cast who also deliver their lines in an overly loud vocal pitch. Kay Johnson, Cromwell's first wife, occasionally displays level-headed practicality as the wife of the lazy, fickle, self-dramatising poet, and Cronjager's mobile camerawork strives vainly to inject some life into the proceedings.

Little Lord Fauntleroy reunited John Cromwell with producer David O. Selznick; it was the first of two expensive re-makes of silent vehicles that they were to produce as a team after Cromwell left RKO. Both film versions of *Fauntleroy* adhered very closely to the original simple story; Cromwell's 1936 one relied on characterisation with a minimum of incident, but with the *implication* of expensive settings to present its effect. In essence, it is one of his happiest works, although it opens with a death; a great deal of the feeling drawn out by the film is evoked by the sheer professionalism of Freddie Bartholomew (e.g., his delighted expression on seeing his present of a penny farthing bicycle, or the series of touching farewells before his departure for England). His innocence provides him with an instant belief in the goodness of his crusty, bigoted grandfather, and shields him against his American friend's anti-British feelings. He wins over his grandfather (Sir C. Aubrey Smith) with the forthright sincerity of his expression (e.g., expressing surprise: "You *don't* wear your coronet all the time?"), and equally endears himself to the local people with his kindness. Arriving at his new home, he feels an immediate empathy with his grandfather's dog ("He knows how I feel"). (Kim Stanley's only childhood companion in *The Goddess* is a cat; Eleanor Parker's spell in prison during *Caged* reaches a crisis after she finds a kitten and tries to hide it from the matron). Since Freddie Bartholomew's beliefs are based on loving innocence, he comes to no harm (whereas Stanley's dreams founder because of their basis of lack of love, while Parker's innocence is corrupted by the system).

When Bartholomew's right to the title is challenged, C. Aubrey Smith reproaches the lawyer, Faversham (Henry Stephen-

Una O'Connor listens as Dolores Costello gives Freddie
Bartholomew a present in LITTLE LORD FAUNTLEROY

son), for "hovering over the boy like a bird of ill omen" (cf.
Zapt hovering in the background disapproving of the King's drink-
ing in *The Prisoner of Zenda* (1937); Davis circling Howard to
deceive him in *Of Human Bondage*). The alternative heir's mother is described as "obviously uneducated and openly mercenary"
—a description that could equally well apply to Stanley's mother
in the first chapter of *The Goddess*, who rejects her child in favour of a good time. Although these illustrations come from several scriptwriters, and are therefore obviously not connected, it
is possible that they stem as much from Cromwell as from the
player; certainly there seems to be a connection in the contrasted

77

lighting of women in his films, here represented by C. Aubrey Smith's meeting with "Dearest" (Dolores Costello), which is softly lit to match her character, whereas the meeting with the fake heir's mother is sharply lit with the hard, flat images underlining her toughness: significantly she moves restlessly around the room during the interview, while "Dearest" remains seated and composed.

Cromwell's eye for correct casting is confirmed by the strong presence of Hollywood's "English Colony" in the supporting roles; his success in obtaining such a winning and confident performance from young Freddie Bartholomew was echoed in later years by the playing of Roddy McDowall in *Son of Fury* (1942) and Richard Lyon in *Anna and the King of Siam* (1946). All in all, *Little Lord Fauntleroy* is a well-balanced, unsophisticated work that adheres closely to its source, but one whose fluid camera style establishes cinematic quality rather than a sense of filmed literature.

Banjo on My Knee (1936) was a complete change of pace. A riverboat yarn, it came out the same year as James Whale's remake of *Show Boat* which starred an old Cromwell favourite, Irene Dunne. The majority of the film takes place in night sequences, so that the impression of impending gloom and misery runs throughout, with a constant pattern of circumstantial meetings or misunderstandings recurrently separating the leading players. A thin plot is strengthened by the inclusion of half a dozen musical interludes, one of which, in the form of a full rendition of "St. Louis Blues," verbally echoes the situation of the heroine, Pearl (Barbara Stanwyck), as well as displaying a strong visual likeness to several of the numbers in *Show Boat* with the staging of the number involving lines of negroes loading a boat as their womenfolk hang out washing in a tenement block and the lead singer sits on the stairs in the centre of the set. The leisurely plot development gives ample scope to the comic antics of Walter

Left to right, producer Nunnally Johnson, Walter Brennan, Tony Martin, Barbara Stanwyck, John Cromwell and Buddy Ebsen pose for the camera while making BANJO ON MY KNEE

Brennan, especially his arrival in New Orleans to "get his family back" after rowing up the river for two weeks; his landing, with the one-man-band contraption that he plays, attracts an instant following of kids and eventually leads to his becoming a cabaret star!

The river people are viewed as caricatures in the scenes depicting their mistrust of the land folk, and their cabaret appearances come over as freak shows rather than an expression of any genuine feeling for them. Camera movement is inhibited apart from the occasional pan or tracking shot, and the film abounds with medium two shots. Pearl is confined to suffering, apart from an initial and a closing display of strong personality, and as a barely literate "hired girl" is at a social disadvantage because she seems not to be expected to have any strength of character; thus she has to verbally defend her susceptibility to the *compliments* of a travelling salesman (Walter Catlett), and her frustration over the constant absences of her husband. Her hysterical outburst, when he finally comes back from sea to turn a welcoming party into a riot, falls in line with the sentiments of other Cromwell heroines who are losers, while Ernie (Joel McCrea) comes on so strong with the bull-headed male chauvinism as her husband ("I'm ordering you to stay here till I send for you") that there is little room left for any further characterisation.

Walter Brennan steals the honours, forever endeavouring to play "St. Louis Blues" as a form of mating encouragement to the young lovers so that he can become a grandfather. His aim is achieved after a great deal of determined effort since nothing ever comes easily to the people in Cromwell's films, and ambition often cloaks failure or death for commoners or even Ruritanian royalty.

*   *   *

Selznick's appreciation of audience tastes led him to ignore warnings of doom if he revived *The Prisoner of Zenda,* which was considered to be a dated Ruritanian drama. He fully realised that casting would be a major factor in the film's success or failure, and later admitted that he would not have considered the project had Ronald Colman not been under contract to him. He assigned Cromwell to direct because of his skill with actors and for his ability to work within a budget (a quality that endeared him to Selznick).

Relations between Cromwell and his leading lady, Madeleine Carroll, were strained from the start; Colman had one bad side photographically speaking so this had to be taken into account during the writing of the script. Then Madeleine Carroll ap-

John Cromwell at work on THE PRISONER OF ZENDA with
David Niven, Ronald Colman and (seated) C. Aubrey Smith

proached Cromwell, claiming a similar problem with the same
side!

"I called on Jimmy Howe [the cameraman], and asked him
if she had a bad side, and he said: "You couldn't fault her if you
stood her on her head!" So I went back to her, pointing out how
ridiculous it was and that we wouldn't be able to shoot the picture if she had the same side as Colman. After that, she would
not speak to me for the rest of the picture."

The fluid style of the finished work makes it surprising to find
that John Cromwell was not the only director involved in the
film. The charm and delicacy of the scene between Rassendyll
and Princess Flavia after the coronation impersonation as he deftly

quizzes "the tow-headed little scarecrow" about his (i.e. the King's) treatment of her as they grew up together, or the natural, honest quality of her love for him, revealed during the ball sequence (when Madeleine Carroll's brilliant underplaying allows her to make the line, "I've never been in love before," work as a devastating virginal demonstration of her trust and feelings) are so effectively achieved by Cromwell (and partially by Selznick's insistence on the actress shedding her traditional make-up), that it is puzzling to learn that Selznick insisted in bringing in George Cukor to film the final scene in which Flavia renounces her love for Rassendyll in favour of her obligations as Queen.

The camerawork is in keeping with the overall style (cross-cutting between Colman and Carroll, filming over alternate shoulders for the frontal closeups, which brings to mind an earlier sequence when Hentzau [Douglas Fairbanks Jr.] takes advantage of a partially open door to force himself on an edgy Antoinette [Mary Astor], who has just helped Rassendyll enter the castle in a bid to rescue the King). However, Cukor presses Carroll into strong reactions, widening her eyes and raising her voice; actions that are not in keeping with the gentle tone of her performance. The action scenes also raise a question of authorship; the fencing sequences are abrupt, and more realistic than most of the other action pieces. Woody Van Dyke was called in to reshoot the death of Black Michael (Raymond Massey) and the duel between Rassendyll and Hentzau during the course of which there is a realistic visual shock as a henchman is run through, and his body falls into a well, intended as a burial place for the King. Just prior to this scene, Cromwell filmed Johann (Byron Foulger) dropping the drawbridge to let Zapt (C. Aubrey Smith) and Fritz (David Niven) into the castle to aid Rassendyll; Hentzau appears and clubs Johann to death (the blows are rained down on the off-screen figure of Johann). Thus Cromwell's presentation of violence would appear to be one of suggestion; yet earlier in the film when Hentzau makes a fruitless attempt on Rassendyll's life, whipping around as his knife misses the target, leaping out of the window and vaulting onto his horse which successfully clears the wall in a hail of bullets, the spontaneity, rhythm and excitement of the sequence belie Selznick's poor opinion of Cromwell's abilities as an action director, especially as Cromwell remembers filming this particular take.

Elegance and style are evident in the relish with which the characters embrace or bitterly oppose the tenets of love, honour and duty that lie at the heart of the story (e.g., Zapt's overriding concern for the welfare of the Crown, verbally and visually indicated in a typical Cromwell *motif* as he strides angrily around the room as Fritz, Rassendyll and the King are getting drunk on the eve of the Coronation; Flavia's renunciation; or the introduction of Hentzau, swaggering into Black Michael's presence, gloriously bedecked and insolently posturing with a cigarette, later betraying his caddish nature by publicly implying an illicit affair between himself and Antoinette, Michael's official mistress). The pomp and splendour of the Coronation is indulged to the hilt with insets of trumpeters and cannon salutes adding to the rich costuming and splendour; the same set (economically) serves as the ballroom with a marvellous establishing shot as Rassendyll and Flavia enter and the camera pulls back, sweeping away from them as they descend three flights of a marble staircase and make their way to the centre of the room between two flanking lines of courtiers; as the music begins, a variety of camera angles gives the suggestion of depth to the room.

Yet another example of Cromwell's visual elegance occurs as Michael and Hentzau bargain with one another in deep armchairs in front of a blazing fireplace. The voices carry across, and with each assertion or counter-claim, the proposer leans forward in view of the camera, stationed at the back of the chairs, only to sink back out of sight as the other person retorts and claims the view. Jealousy and treachery as feminine characteristics appear with Antoinette's betrayal of Michael (although her real motive is love), and with the housekeeper's complicity in drugging the King, and they were to remain as important iconographical factors in Cromwell's later work (e.g. the Frances Farmer role in *Son of Fury* and Lizabeth Scott in *Dead Reckoning*.)

* * *

Cromwell's next assignment was to make an English-speaking version of Duvivier's highly successful French thriller, *Pepe Le Moko* (1936), which the producer Walter Wanger used as a springboard to launch Hedy Lamarr's career in America. James Wong Howe's photographic skill reproduced the high quality of the original, while Cromwell drew polished performances from Boyer, Gene Lockhart and Joseph Calleia, after a shaky opening with Paul Harvey (!) cast as a French policeman. John Howard Lawson's tight, logical script centred around the duel of wits betwen Boyer as an international thief and Calleia as a wily cop trying to lure him out of his refuge in the Casbah, and it was far more effective than John Berry's 1948 musical re-make, *Casbah*.

After his "copy job" for Wanger, and a fruitless project beginning *The Adventures of Marco Polo* (1938, Archie Mayo, John Ford) for Sam Goldwyn but being fired after a week for not informing Goldwyn of his intended shooting schedule, Cromwell returned to the stage, directing a play with Fredric March and Florence Eldridge before accepting an offer from Selznick to film *Made for Each Other* (1939) with a stellar cast including James Stewart and Carole Lombard. Selznick was busily preparing *Gone with the Wind*, but in spite of divided attention *Made for Each Other* shares the simple narrative style, and smooth, polished finish of their other producer/director collaborations once they had left R.K.O.

The plot follows the development of a marriage, charting the emotional high and low points against a background that intermingles the trivial and traumatic events and people which jointly or individually cause familiar problems for any young couple. This emotional transition is depicted in direct, frequently funny and often moving terms; any tendency towards sentimentality is restrained by the natural acting, the comic interludes in the form of situation jokes or "tongue-in-the-cheek" satire, and the technical assurance behind Cromwell's direction. For instance, he adapts a highly melodramatic style for the birth of the baby with low-key lighting pinpointing Stewart's agitation as he wakens suddenly in a darkened room, rushes along murky corridors and flings open a door to be confronted with an empty bed when he has obviously expected to find Lombard asleep there; skilful camera placement, and the odd tilted angle shot backed by an emotively pulsating score, gently rib the actor and the melodramatics of the scene in terms of its normal presentation in films of this type. Similarly, the highly emotive impact of an over-the-shoulder close-up of Lombard as they embrace after expressing their doubts about the wisdom of a decision to marry, occurs again many years later in *The Goddess*, but in the latter context it takes the form of a savage parody of the romantic *genre*.

The incompetence of Stewart's office rival, Carter (Donald Briggs); the dishonesty of his boss, Judge Dolittle (Charles Coburn), and the meddling of his mother (Lucile Watson) are all redeemed by a particular act of goodness or kindness; thus they do not carry the vindictive force of purely dramatic characters in other Cromwell films, although Judge Dolittle's weedy daughter (formerly considered engaged to Stewart) is significantly brunette in direct contrast to the blonde, light-natured Lombard (the same colour contrast recurs throughout Cromwell's films to a point of obsession).

The simplicity of the story allows for a great deal of insight into the characters, and for an unusual amount of flexibility in the cast's playing. Lombard is casual and very human: gritting her teeth and quietly repeating, "I won't say anything, I won't say anything!" as her mother-in-law's nagging touches a raw nerve in a period of stress; her daily letters to Stewart in the early stages of the film are an endearingly romantic personal touch as well as an inspired lead-in for a gag involving the embarrassed husband and the gruff Judge Dolittle, but above all her ambition for her young lawyer husband is practical (a similar scene in *Abe Lincoln in Illinois* presents Mary Todd rehearsing her proposed entrapment of Lincoln in front of her outraged family). Lombard's ambition is not to drive her husband to great heights, merely to

John Cromwell, Carole Lombard and James Stewart
pose on the set of MADE FOR EACH OTHER

make him stand up for his rights instead of being a self-confessed mouse! Her quiet understatement when an argumentative Stewart staggers in after a bender both prevents a row and leads to a closer bond between them.

The role is perfectly tailored for Stewart as the gangling, awkward young husband; the puzzled expression that crosses his face, when it is suggested that his sudden marriage on a business trip will upset his employer since it was generally assumed that he was engaged unofficially to the Judge's only daughter, indicates the mixture of innocence, naivety and perhaps immaturity. His clanger when he is entertaining the Judge, Miss Dolittle and Carter at his home prior to the announcement of a new partner for the firm is absolutely typical of the character. Backing into the lounge, he urges Lombard to hurry with her dressing as "Granite-puss will be here any minute," only to discover that the Judge is standing right behind him! His New Year depression, after a humiliating evening at a class reunion when, as the former most promising prospect, he finds that he has fallen behind his companions, which in turn leads him into doubting the wisdom of marriage, is given an unconscious irony in the face of the coming events in that year of 1939.

Charles Coburn shifts attitudes like a chameleon; gruff, fatherly, penny-pinching (as he dismisses Stewart from his office after talking him into a decrease in pay, he is heard clinching a property deal for a house on Park Avenue), but strangely blind to the superior abilities of Stewart—the suggestion being that he is susceptible to influence from his daughter with regard to the advancement of male staff. The honours for the polished momentum of the film belong as much to John Cromwell as the players for it is he who tied all the loose ends, together with his editor. The impact of a drunken reveller unfurling a "Happy New Year" whistle across Lombard's face, obscuring her reaction as a doctor informs her and Stewart that their baby is desperately ill with pneumonia, carries the same symbolic weight and effect as the masked drunks who break into Laverne's hotel room on New Year's Eve as she is pouring out her unhappy story to the sympathetic reporter in Sirk's *Tarnished Angels*. Reality is ever present in Cromwell's work, surfacing even in his lightest offerings.

Carole Lombard also appeared in *In Name Only* (1939), giving a moving performance as the other woman in Cary Grant's life. The melodrama hinges on rather too many coincidences, but it again illustrates Cromwell's skill in welding together his material.

He controls the performances, modulating them to the tone of the scenes. The opening sequences, set in rural Connecticut (Cromwell's own home state for many years) with Lombard mutely fishing, literally sparkles with the soft focus of the photography and the art of Lombard's mime. The jaunty score recurs throughout the Connecticut scenes as Grant and Lombard meet, go on a picnic, and fall in love; the restful quality of the meetings, with Lombard describing the need for conversation as an unnecessary nervous habit with some people, and Grant clowning in the best Hawksian tradition, are in sharp contrast to the scenes at his home. His wife, played by Kay Francis, generally wears black; the score is sombre; she and his parents are constantly isolated in medium shots, or the camera tracks after Francis capturing her nervous, restless energy as she paces around. (In a reprise of the Lubitsch touch with doors*), Grant moves from

---

* "In *The Marriage Circle* when Monte Blue leaves Marie Prevost to emphasise the finality of his leaving her, Lubitsch has him go out of door after door after door, until he is finally in the street, glad to be out of that trap." [From "The Lubitsch Touch," page 100, by Herman G. Weinberg.]

room to room, placing their solid frame between himself and his wife and family.

The premise of the film is stated in a confrontation between Lombard and her man-hating sister, Laura, when Lombard insists that people should try to retain their romantic illusions. Cromwell's attitude to his "soap opera" material differs from the other artists such as Cukor, Borzage and Stahl with whom I linked him earlier in that he is basically anti-romantic, playing down sentimentality and opting for realism and practicality instead. He is not a moral realist like John Farrow, whose anarchist in *Five Came Back* (1939) is allowed to play God in choosing which of the passengers must live or die after a plane crash in the jungle since he is the most objective of all the characters.

Cary Grant's natural flippancy is seen as naivety and immaturity, and his love for Lombard can only work out when they are both prepared to face their problem practically and realistically. They have to fight both Kay Francis's insincerity and possessive severity as well as his parents' (and the family doctor's) moral austerity. The narrowness and conformity of the latter's world is suggested by their constant appearance in formal groupings. At the same time Lombard has to face up to her sister's insinuations that she is placing herself and her child in an untenable situation, and will be let down just as Laura was in the past.

Kay Francis's obsession (Lombard: "She loves you in some way I don't understand") with keeping Grant is similar to that of Barbara O'Neil in Stahl's *When Tomorrow Comes* (1939), but O'Neil proves to be insane, whereas Francis's motive is finally revealed as greed, like Mildred in *Of Human Bondage,* when she confronts Lombard outside Grant's hospital room. She has already indicated to Grant that she wed him for "what went with him" and she then tells Lombard: "Some day his father is going to die." Innocence once again proves triumphant since the father (Charles

Coburn) is standing behind her at the time.

Cromwell neatly injects a note of pessimism into the buoyant memory of love which fills Grant and Lombard as he takes her back from New York to the Connecticut cottage where she was living when they first met, thinking his wife has gone to Paris to divorce him. After a witty exchange about Grant's lurid taste in wallpaper ("Funny, it looked nice rolled up"), the gardener mentions Francis by name, immediately bringing Lombard down. They embrace in a medium-long shot, seen through two open doors (reminding one of the use of doors earlier in Grant's home) and, from that point on, a *Back Street* finale seems inevitable with Francis on the attack, Lombard depressed ("This is today, and this is all we're ever going to get") and wearing black as Grant goes to pieces in a *Lost Weekend* type binge before falling seriously ill in a sleazy hotel where the manager makes a play for Lombard. But, with all her illusions shattered, she makes a final romantic gesture to the memory of her love for Grant by agreeing to the head doctor's suggestion that she tells him what he wants to hear: the credo of the romantic film always demands that the heroine be put in the position of making the final, noble sacrifice. Then, in this case, Fate steps in on the right side.

Cromwell's perfect judging of mood and his skill in blending contrasting performances nearly brings it off. Grant is believable, and is able to work in some good comedy routines such as the acid-tongued confrontation with his wife's best "friend," and his rapid fire delivery as the "census man" when he appears on Lombard's New York doorstep after she has fled from Connecticut. Lombard is her unique self; alternating gymnastically between gay charm and noble, dignified self-sacrifice, and the supporting cast perform capably without over-playing despite the temptations offered by the script, but ultimately the film belongs to the grim Kay Francis for moments such as the close of a scene in which she has initially agreed to a divorce, stopping Grant short with the vehemence of her declaration: "I hope you'll both be miserable." Stubborn, obsessive women recur throughout Cromwell's later films, ranging from the sadistic matron in *Caged*, and Kim Stanley's pathetic star in *The Goddess* to the slightly more sympathetic Mary Todd Lincoln, as portrayed by Ruth Gordon in *Abe Lincoln in Illinois* (1940).

Abraham Lincoln had long been a popular figure in historical films; when John Cromwell came to film Robert Sherwood's play about Lincoln, he faced the prospect of following on the heels of John Ford, whose *Young Mr. Lincoln* (1939) had covered much of the same period of Lincoln's life. Cromwell laid greater emphasis on detail and character than Ford, who chose—not unexpectedly—to stress the mythic qualities inherent in the tale of a backwoods lawyer who rose to the highest position in the nation. There are similarities in the casting with Ford using Ward Bond in a rough-neck role that approximates to the Howard Da Silva character in Cromwell's film, but Da Silva is more sympathetic, while Ford also spends more time on the Perry Mason-type court drama and romanticises Ann Rutledge with a graveside eulogy scene.

Cromwell plays down her role, using it as a foil to establish qualities of Lincoln's nature; his wrestling with Da Silva to defend the lady's honour; Abe's self-conscious proposal to Ann when her *fiancé*'s absence in New York makes her the subject of gossip. Raymond Massey is a far less confident Lincoln than Henry Fonda; his lack of ambition, laziness and scepticism are more in keeping with the self-doubting Brigham Young, another biographical study filmed (by Henry Hathaway) in 1940. Ruth Gordon's *début* as Mary Todd, the girl Lincoln was to marry and who forced him to face up to his destiny, is a remarkably astute and cinematic interpretation. One of the highlights of the film is the aforementioned scene in which she maps out her plan of courtship, making it plain she intends to force Lincoln's hand. Like the self-destructive *Goddess* her success leads to her downfall: in this instance, the later loveless years as a paranoid shrew.

Massey in contrast grows in stature before our eyes; Wong Howe's lighting and camera placement complete the illusion by strengthening the gaunt, hungry ambition that has replaced the gawky laziness—particularly in the final sequence with Lincoln standing pensively at the rear of a train taking him East after a moving farewell speech in the gathering dusk (backed by the strains of "John Brown's Body"). As we know his destiny, the affirmation of his decision gives a poignant effect to the emotional core of the ending.

The positive characterisation in *Abe Lincoln in Illinois* was coupled with a strong sense of humour, especially in the earlier segments of the film with Massey meeting Ann Rutledge while catching pigs ("I don't know the name of the pig"), and his hilarious misadventures drilling recruits for a campaign against the Indians; but Cromwell's next project offered little opportunity for humour. In filming Joseph Conrad's *Victory* (1940), he was following distinguished predecessors in Maurice Tourneur and William A. Wellman. He had once again produced a stage version—his first stage production, in fact; while setting this up he had contacted Joseph Conrad's agent regarding the purchase of the dramatic and producing rights, only to find that the former had been assigned to a dramatist named McDonald Hastings.

At first, owing to a misunderstanding on Cromwell's part, he thought that Conrad was working on the adaptation with Hastings; he negotiated and purchased the producing rights without seeing a script, and when the script arrived he was horrified by

The final shot of ABE LINCOLN IN ILLINOIS as Lincoln (Raymond Massey) travels toward his destiny

it as Cromwell had very firm convictions about the dramatisation and Hastings' adaptation did not measure up to them! He wrote to Hastings, who replied giving him short shrift, but, undeterred, Cromwell replied with specific criticisms, sending a copy of the letter to Conrad. Conrad replied that he heartily agreed and understood all Cromwell's objections, but that it was not within his make-up to interfere with what Hastings was trying to do. Both Laurence Irving's London production, using Hastings' script, and Cromwell's version in America were flops, but Cromwell longed for another crack at the property.

"During the first weeks of my contract at Paramount, they made a production of *Victory* entitled *Dangerous Paradise,* which was just deplorable . . . just awful! I mean not only the script, but they had Richard Arlen (remember him?) playing Heyst!! So, when they came to do it again, I thought now maybe I can do this and make some sense out of it. I thought I had the ideal cast with one exception: I couldn't get anyone to play the Cockney, and I should have insisted on their getting somebody from England. The man we had, to be fair, was a pretty good character actor, but nothing like he should have been . . . it was such a rich character. Then, Mr. Hardwicke whom I knew—or thought I knew—pretty well: I don't know what the hell happened to him. He just conked out on me entirely, and I felt gave no indication of what the part was about. I don't know what the devil was bothering him, or what he was going through at the time, because there seemed to be no effort on his part.

Again we were faced with the same sort of situation we had on *Of Human Bondage* (where we had to have six previews to eliminate bad laughs). Heyst, under the dominance of a father who instilled these ideas in him so thoroughly, was the type of man who only wanted to find an island in the South Seas, live there and see the world go by . . . it was enough to make primitive audiences say: "That ain't the kind of hero we want."

Cromwell and Fredric March tried hard to back out of *So Ends Our Night* because America had just entered the war and they both felt the film would be redundant, but Cromwell has happy memories of its making: "It was one of the best scripts I've ever had . . . but there was a production problem in that in the usual picture you have somewhere in the neighbourhood of seventy-eighty sets, and you have a budget that fits it! We had 126 sets, but were fortunate in obtaining William Cameron Menzies as designer. With the use of his continuity sketches, we were able to work from a basis of pre-arranged shots, like that of Freddy March entering the hospital in Berlin. Menzies designed a back wall, about 15 feet high, and used a piece of handpainted glass right up close to the camera to continue the wall with a great cove and magnificent ceiling. All this was done on half of a stage with white 'compo' board, so you had a completely white floor and back wall with an attendant in the foreground . . . a terrific production shot. But the film was not a success—except to me, as I thought it one of my best."

Son of Fury contains the two extremes of Cromwell's career; unfortunately, in the confrontation between good taste, a lavish budget and atmospheric characterisation on the one hand and subservience to studio influence on the other, the latter proves to be the stronger factor. There is a particularly good flavour to the detail and atmosphere of the opening Wiltshire sequences, and Roddy McDowall performs admirably. Then the plot becomes prominent, and the hero returns to primitivism to gain wealth in order to return to England to reclaim his rightful title; if it sounds familiar, it should, as it was one of the stock Twentieth Century-Fox costume picture yarns (cf. Hathaway's *The Black Rose* or Delmer Daves's *Treasure of the Golden Condor*, the latter being an early Fifties re-make of *Son of Fury*).

At first, the South Seas idyll with Gene Tierney modelling a vintage bikini and displaying an astonishing facility for learning pidgin English overnight, seems like an unhappy but transitory intrusion, but after the hero's first love is revealed to be hand in glove with nasty George Sanders, he spurns her only to return to the South Seas.

Although the decor is elaborate, Cromwell makes no use, visual or otherwise, of the lavish settings, unlike his earlier Selznick films; the Sanders character shows no visible ageing while Roddy McDowall grows up into Tyrone Power over an explicit time lapse; while the action scenes, oddly enough for a period film, all consist of fisticuffs with the climactic sequence in the vein of *Wait until Dark* or *Straw Dogs* with an apparently unconscious villain making a shock recovery. The two protagonists then proceed to struggle on, systematically removing all the existing sources of light in the room until Power emerges triumphant.

"*Son of Fury* was definitely a studio project, and I never cared for the story much for the same reasons as yourself. I liked very much working with Power and particularly with Gene Tierney. I had an experience with her when she first came to Hollywood; I had been sent a test of hers while she was still under contract to Columbia. I thought the test extraordinary, and she and her mother came to see me about it. Then I discovered I had met her mother during my second year on the stage. Her mother had been about seventeen and lived in New York where I had to go every August to get a job. Now her daughter was seventeen and breathtakingly beautiful. Gene had been at Columbia for six months but had done nothing except 'leg art'. What could they do? I told them, if they could get out of the contract, to do so, go back to New York and get her into the theatre to learn her business. When she had first come to see me, I had asked her what she wanted to do and she had answered: 'To be a fine actress.'

That's why I gave her the advice I had, explaining that after five years she would undoubtedly know something and would probably be able to have something to say about what she did. Some time later I saw that she was playing a small part in a new play by James Thurber called "The Male Animal." When I was in New York I called to see my old friend, Elliott Nugent, who was acting in the play, and saw Gene backstage. I congratulated her, and several months later saw another notice in the paper to the effect that Gene Tierney had just been signed to a long term contract by Fox, and was being prepared to appear in the lead in a new production. I murmured to myself: 'Goodbye, fine actress!' I never saw her in a film that I liked until *Son of Fury* and I think that was because I worked so hard to get her to stop acting and be simple." [Letter to the author dated 15th October 1973].

* * *

After the release of *Gone with the Wind* (1939) and *Rebecca* (1940), David O. Selznick re-shuffled the organization of Selznick International and formed David O. Selznick Productions, Inc. Much of his time was taken up with the search for a new project, and also with the launching of his new *protegée*, Jennifer Jones, in a Fox film directed by Henry King, *The Song of Bernadette* (1943). Having achieved the latter aim, he decided to cast her in a major role in his next production, *Since You Went Away* (1944), for which he had fashioned a screenplay from a story by Margaret Buell Wilder, and he invited John Cromwell to direct.

From Selznick's recently published memos, it is apparent that he did not much like the construction and characterisation of the original story. He re-wrote it, updating the period and expanding it to cover a broad canvas of America at war. Dedicated to the bastion of the American Dream, "the unconquerable fortress of 1943—the American family," the finished film ran just under three hours and it is undoubtedly one of the most superior, polished and effective propaganda works to emerge from the American cinema during the Second World War.

A "ten handkerchief" weepie—at times banal, sentimental (constantly sentimental, in fact) and thoroughly gripping—it is also extremely entertaining and emotionally moving because it is based on *honest* feeling. Time and again it sparks off a true response from its audience to a *clichéd* or over-exposed situation as it is played with such genuine, tender conviction by an extremely large cast. As in other Cromwell/Selznick collaborations, the narrative moves in a series of incidents or chapters but it is so slickly welded that one hardly notices this device during a viewing. The direction, the camera movements and, to a great extent, Max Steiner's score are understated, allowing the performances fluidity, natural warmth and a conviction that belies acting—a quality that is seldom achieved with such a predominantly starry cast.

This conviction that the performers are real people as opposed to actors in parts fits into the overall conception of the film; i.e. when direction, camera movements and scoring are *not* understated, as in the marvellous set piece of the dance in a huge hangar with the camera gliding, swooping, panning and tracking back into long shots such as the reverse angle perspective (seen from behind and through a vast decorative "Wings of Eagles" sign) as the spotlights swing and sway over the dancing throng; or the lateral track as Colbert and Moorehead move down the highlighted corridor of a bar while snatches of conversation from the people seated at the bar tables (in dim low-key lighting) provide a commentary on the feelings of people at war. The latter effect is repeated with equal emotional effect at the railway station as the troops prepare to leave. The love scene on the porch between Jones and Robert Walker when he talks about his expulsion from West Point is particularly striking in its use of shadow and calls

An impregnable fortress of 1943: the American Family. Daughters Jennifer Jones and Shirley Temple listen to their mother, Claudette Colbert, read aloud from a letter which her father has sent after his departure for war in SINCE YOU WENT AWAY

to mind Selznick's instructions to James Wong Howe for the terrace scene in *The Prisoner of Zenda* where he asked for real night shooting that would not avoid casting figures in dark shadows but would retain enough light to catch the expression on their faces. Also Jennifer Jones's playing in the early stages seems doll-like, her movements and delivery are awkward, but in the light of her subsequent acceleration into maturity when Walker dies in action, this seems justified: the romantic girl who scorns her younger sister's suggestion that they take in a boarder as Communistic until it is clear that he will be an *officer* (hence a romantic possibility) does indeed grow in stature before our eyes, clumsily endeavouring to heal the breach between Walker and his crusty grandfather (Monty Woolley, in a similar role to that of *The Man Who Came to Dinner,* but here being upstaged by a bulldog!), growing out of her crush on Tony, her mother's ex-suitor, to blossom as she falls in love with Walker, only to have to face his death. Her hysterical attack on the vulgarly thoughtless society hostess, Emily (Agnes Moorehead), is at once a beautifully controlled piece of acting and the crowning point of her characterisation.

Hattie McDaniel as the faithful maid, Robert Walker and Guy Madison as two nervous young men, a remarkably dignified and restrained Lionel Barrymore as a preacher, and a host of other players all register strongly; Shirley Temple displays her professional competence in moving from coy, cute children to a cheerful teenager with consummate ease, matched only by the sheer skill of Colbert and Joseph Cotten, neither of whom have ever been so precise in drawing their roles, before or since. The sincerity of Colbert's voice on the soundtrack as she recounts her inner turmoil while wandering numbly around her empty house after sending her husband off to war, has a winning credibility that instantly makes one accept her as Anne, mother of two girls, who in the coming months will have to cope with all the household chores since an officer's wage cannot cover the maid's pay; uncertainly, she will have to take in a lodger and cope with his whims and tantrums, put up with the shallowness of her "friend" Emily, guide her daughters through illness and decisions *re* going to college or taking a war job. She has some relief and aid from a close family friend, Tony, with whom she has a Flaubertian relationship; she knows his verbal passes are just words of friendship and comfort; she *is* the sort of woman who might nod off during a newsreel and miss seeing a glimpse of her husband on the battle front, and who might miss a cherished chance of seeing him between trains because she could not make the cross-country connection in time. Mrs. Average (middle-class) Woman whose husband is one of the many Mr. Averages who are missing in action, she has to find the strength to accept her lot, and to help her eldest daughter face the same situation; she has the tact to effect a reconciliation between Walker and Woolley, only for Fate to cruelly intervene at the last gasp. After all this, she berates herself during the confrontation with Emily for not doing enough, and takes on a war job!

Cotten convinces not through his presence as an actor, but by sound development of his character: glib, self-confident, but understanding in his humouring of Jones's crush on him and objective about the war itself ("Privates—these are the boys that do the fighting, and largely because of their dreams of girls like you"), and foreseeingly cynical about the outcome with his speech concerning their hopes for a better life after the war; mocking his own role as an outsider, by suggesting he would look funny making verbal passes at Colbert when they were both aged in wheelchairs after she askes him to remain the same forever.

The script does avoid the more unpleasant details of war, or rather it pares them down to their minimum. The meeting with the Mahoney boy at the dance, when Colbert agrees to ask her husband about finding the boy a job in advertising after the war, is followed by news of his death on a training flight; the poignancy of the situation is underlined when she and the girls see the boy's father in the cinema leaving during a newsreel about the bravery of flyers. Also, little is seen of Jones's work as a nurse's aid, while hoarding and black marketeering are referred to in dialogue only. But this would seem to be legitimate as the film is about families in war, not the war itself.

It is tempting to see the hand of Selznick behind many of the film's virtues but to over-credit him would be an injustice to Cromwell's succinct manipulation of the players and of the resources of the brilliant technicians who combined their talents to create the film. In many other films, the ornamentation such as the fairy tale frescoes on the milk bar wall or the mural of nurses, soldiers and the Cross as Jennifer Jones takes her oath as a nurse's aid, would be considered lavish in the extreme, but in the context of *Since You Went Away*, William L. Pereira's production design and Mark-Lee Kirk's settings are quite acceptable, indeed fitting. Had Cromwell never made another film, his reputation as an outstanding Hollywood professional could have survived entirely on the strength of *Since You Went Away*.

*　*　*

He is very fond of the two films that followed *Since You Went Away*. *The Enchanted Cottage*, made for RKO, was a tender romantic drama, adapted and updated from Arthur Wing Pinero's famous play, telling how a badly disfigured war hero and an ugly duckling find complete spiritual rehabilitation and happiness through mutual love and understanding with the aid of a blind composer. It was recounted in flashback, and handled with perception and feeling. Then came *Anna and the King of Siam*, a demonstration of Cromwell's craftsmanship that won Oscars for the black-and-white photography and the art direction. A teacher comes to instruct the King of Siam's children and copes with the intolerant King; the narrative is presented as a series of incidents in which she seeks to guide the King in matters of state and house-

John Cromwell confers with Herbert Marshall, Robert Young and Dorothy McGuire during a break from shooting on THE ENCHANTED COTTAGE

hold. It is notable for its non-reliance on spectacle and avoidance of light relief, with Cromwell's usual insistence on character to the fore as in the vivid cameo of Dunne failing to dissuade the King from burning runaway wife Linda Darnell at the stake, which is particularly effectively mounted.

A difficult period for John Cromwell began in 1947. He made *Night Song*, a disaster about a blind composer falling in love with a rich society girl who feigns blindness to win him and pay for an operation to restore his sight. He finds out the truth, but love conquers all in an unbelievable film in which the musical background is often more interesting. *Dead Reckoning* marked a return to the world of crime:

"There were a lot of conditions of history behind *Dead Reckoning* that influenced the film. I had put Humphrey Bogart on the stage when he was a kid; he used to hang around the Playhouse Theatre with young Bill Brady and another kid named 'Bull' Durham; they sat in on rehearsals just from interest, and a situation came up with one of those comedies when a part is underwritten and you can't get a good boy to do it so you compromise. That's what this was; somebody thought of Bogart, who at the time was the most responsible, the most charming . . . the best of the three kids. He was, of course, goggle-eyed to do it, and I think he said to me once: 'Mr. Cromwell, what do I do? Do I face out to the audience when I speak my lines, or do I talk to the characters?' I went through all these things with him, but the play was an awful flop, yet he went on with his career. Subsequently, I met him two or three times socially in Hollywood, but the idea of working together didn't arise until Harry Cohn had to lend a couple of his people to Warner Brothers, and he was smart enough to do an exchange for a picture with Bogart.

"Warners stalled for some years, then called him up and said: 'O.K. You can have Bogart from this date to that.' So there was a time limit on making the picture; Bogart had the right to pick the director and the story, and they suggested all these names to him, until finally, out of curiosity on his part when my name was mentioned, he agreed. He had never quarrelled with me, and I felt the same way although we had no story. They had the usual pile of stuff they always had handy to see whom they could pass it off onto . . . I finally got this one, a noxious sort of thing, but I felt perhaps we could make something of it."

The resulting picture, about a tough veteran of the Second World War finding the killer of an old Army pal, offered Bogart a strong characterisation but was hampered by the inadequacy of Lizabeth Scott as the villainess.

Cromwell's name was mentioned several times during the hearings of the Committee of Un-American Activities investigation into the influence of Communists in the Hollywood film industry, when ten writers and directors were cited and convicted of contempt for failing to answer certain questions about their affiliations.

"I was nothing but what I called a 'liberal' Democrat with no interest in what we call popular politics until we came to the advent of Roosevelt's third term, and then I got concerned because I felt it was essential that he was re-elected. I joined, and worked pretty consistently for, a small organisation called the Hollywood Democratic Committee, eventually finding myself the head of the thing. It was formed to raise ideas and money for Roosevelt's re-election, but it was a silly organisation in that its greatest effort seemed to be in the collection of dues from the 3,000 members!

"But I began to feel the pressures alright. There's an amusing story . . . I had asked my agent to find out whether I was on a list of 200 names which was supposed to be universally circulated in all the big studios, and he did what he could to find out, and said: 'Absolutely not.' And I felt this was virtually a clearance because my name was on the local state list and had cropped up very often. So I got this contract from RKO, the best contract I had in Hollywood, which allowed for one picture a year with a proviso of conditions over twenty-three weeks*, and my agent was smart enough to make this the catch in the contract. If they daubed the walls or anything and I went over contract, my salary would treble! About two weeks after I had signed, Hughes bought RKO . . . and the complete freedom from inter-studio politics went up in smoke. Dudley Nichols, one of the best screen-writers in the business, had a reputation that was rather tinged by this sort of thinking, so he and virtually all the rest just forgot their contracts and walked out of the studios because they knew it was useless to stay there.

---

* With a proviso of conditions relating to additional salary etc., if the production ran over twenty-three weeks.

"I thought about it very seriously, but I could not afford it at my time of life, and I didn't think they could harm me much, so I stayed. But the first thing that happened was that, without word of warning, they reverted to the old RKO system by which they just sent me a script and said: 'This will be your next assignment.' I looked at the script, and the name of it was *I Married a Communist,* and I thought this was kind of funny. I read it, and I had never read such a bad script in my life; the more I thought about it, the more convinced I became that it could never be made. So I decided to stick it out; the next thing that happened was that they assigned to the story, as the writer, one of the worst 'witch hunters' in Hollywood, and I saw that was pretty deliberate.

"I found I could dope out just when this whole thing started because at M-G-M at that time there was a coterie of writers and different people that were convinced of this Communist idea; they were all hung together and one of them, a well known writer, was a great friend of Hughes and he had come to Hughes and said: 'Look, if you can't get rid of Cromwell, I'll tell you how to do it. There's a script going around, you can buy it for about $15,000. Give it to Cromwell. He'll refuse to do it, and there you go.'

"So we came to the first meeting on the script, and in these kind of set-ups where you buy a completed first script, you usually start in with the writers. They tell you what they intend to do with it, and in this case it did not need any introduction on my part to get the writer going. He began with a great deal of assurance, being a very cocky character . . . also a perfect lush. He made no reference to knowing about my reputation, but I knew that he did. I followed his build-up closely, realising that he was saying nothing but tying himself in knots. I countered him by logically suggesting that if we did this, this and that, you would create situation x, but on top of that you had situation y, so eventually you would end up with no story at all! It was as simple as that, and I could do it all off the cuff!

"He struggled out of it with great difficulty as it was *so* apparent, and he immediately suggested we break for lunch. He got back late after a couple of drinks, and seeing how it would go, I closed up tighter than a drum. Three or four days later, he was 'ill' and, after the accounts department checked my contract and realised they would soon be paying me three times my salary, he was taken off the picture. After sitting it out a while longer, they found this young fellow from the "Los Angeles Times," who was very anxious to get into pictures (he did later, but was killed in a plane crash with Mike Todd, while writing Todd's biography).

"Anyway, he came on the picture, I liked him as he was very eager and wanted to learn all he could, to contribute all he could. I knew I could not take him quietly aside and say: 'Look, this picture can never be made. It is just an impossible story.' So I tried my best to help him by teaching him a few of the elements of picture writing. Finally the studio realised it was hopeless; he was having too much difficulty and they could not get anybody else, so they just shelved the picture, and loaned me to Warner Brothers for *Caged*."

* * *

Caged is one of the bitterest films in Cromwell's canon, surpassed only by *The Goddess*. It builds up in a progression of accusations which are structured in terms of their importance. Men are seen as women's downfall; harsh treatment in prison brutalises them; sadism breaks them; official indifference and political chicanery prevents liberal aid; their corruption is completed by their contact with hardened criminals who are themselves victims. Thus the wheel has turned full circle.

Cromwell pulls no punches in outlining this hierarchy, using visual effects and hard-boiled dialogue to the fullest extent, but above all stressing character in the individual performances as a means of stating his case.

Unlike *Son of Fury*, he incorporates studio trademarks—in this case, the hard, flat visual surface and a hyper-evident musical backing long associated with Warner Brothers—without allowing them to interfere with his skilful handling of a strong cast, utilising a minimum of sets to tell his story and make his case. He is on record as strongly believing in casting against type, and here this is represented by the casting of Agnes Moorehead as the sympathetic head warden, whose liberal attempts are completely overshadowed by the huge Hope Emerson as the sadistic matron. The natural sharpness of Moorehead's appearances is toned down to complete the contrast.

The opening shot of a speeding van entering a prison yard, with the mesh window as the only source of light available as the credits unfurl, is typical of the economy and impact with which Cromwell started his later films. The claustrophobic atmosphere is depressingly heightened as the door is flung open with the words: "File out, you tramps. It's the end of the line." Hard, impersonal female warders check the girls in as part of a boring, familiar routine ("Pregnant? Another bill for the State!"); the sound of a passing overhead train transfixes the whole ward, stressing their isolation from the outside world.

Marie (Eleanor Parker), a first offender, is soon made aware of the hierarchy, and the philosophy of the more hardened inmates ("You get tough or you get killed"); she sees a girl go stir crazy, learns that the matron runs a sales centre on the side, and she meets Kitty (Betty Garde), who organises a shop-lifting chain. But Kitty's influence counts for nil when a rich rival, Elvira (Lee Patrick), who is a vice madam, is put in the ward, and encourages the matron to persecute Kitty. Marie changes from an innocent

Bitter irony surrounds the composition of the shot as the
sadistic matron, Hope Emerson, relaxes in her room
during CAGED

girl into a hardened con; losing her baby prematurely, she learns
to defend herself against the matron and a sado-masochistic relationship develops between them, culminating in her hair being
shaved bare after a confrontation over a kitten which had found
its way into the exercise yard. When the matron talks of having
it put down, a riot flares; Cromwell stresses the disruption to the
enclosed routine by employing jump cuts to smashing lights, and
by tilting the camera. Similarly, he uses another camera movement—a long tracking shot—to draw out the tension when Marie

bursts into hysteria, backed by the sound of a clanging prison bell, as the parole board refuse her appeal.

By the time Marie has finished a spell in solitary, she comes out a hard cookie, but the experiences she has lived through give poignancy to Moorehead's final words after she has interviewed Marie, just prior to the girl's release: "She'll be back."

RKO tried to cash in on *Caged*'s success with *The Company She Keeps*, reuniting Cromwell with Lizabeth Scott. It dealt with a parolee, Jane Greer, who steals her probation officer Scott's boyfriend, and helps another parolee steal drugs when she believes the boy-friend is unwilling to marry her. Well cast in the supporting roles, it was patchily written in spite of some punchy dialogue, and Cromwell only occasionally was able to build up to dramatic highspots or give rein to the histrionic abilities of the cast. His career came full circle with the assignment of *The Racket*.

It emerges as a cold, pessimistic gangster film, updated to cover the rise of the Syndicate; the business corporation structure is minutely observed from the brainless thugs, through the crooked bail bondsmen and cops and corrupt judges to the unseen "Man" at the top. Cromwell captures the bland feel of a world in which cars slide menacingly into the frame, characters are isolated in single shots, two-shots represent aggression, and groups an unhappy security. He endows it with touches like Ryan's pacing psychotic, constantly on the brink of explosion into insanity (as in *Dead Reckoning* with the Marvin Miller part), or the use of the camera moving in on closing doors to block out sentimentality (e.g., Mitchum taking a policeman's wife into his office to break the news of her husband's death, when she has called at the station to see him and guessed from an overheard conversation what is happening, is represented by a sob from behind a closed door); an exciting rooftop fight to the death is filmed at night *sans* music; some violence occurs out of the frame, leaving audiences in suspense as to the outcome. There are weaknesses: the sub-plot romance between two material witnesses is weakly played and the pace lags in the police station, but it comes across as a capable entertainment.

The promise of complete freedom with the editing lured Cromwell back to the cinema to make a film about Hollywood. In the intervening years, his only contact had been an acting role in a Kirk Douglas/Susan Hayward vehicle, but he had been active in the theatre. *The Goddess* (1958) is his last major work, and in many respects one of his best films, although it was made against a background of troubles with the front office, and he is far from satisfied with the result. The freedom with editing extended to the first cut, then pressure was indirectly applied through the writer, Paddy Chayefsky, until Cromwell finally walked off the project. The release print runs half the length of his original version, and bears the title: "under the supervision of George Justin."

The film is divided into chapters: the first time a Cromwell film was specifically sub-divided, although many had moved in a similar direction before, just as the circular motif in the construction of the episodes would seem to be an unconscious habit of Cromwell's. Stanley rejects her child with the same words her mother used to reject her; she starts to understand her first husband's loneliness on meeting him twenty years later. Her rejection of him (he, mentioning combat duty: "I hope I get killed"; she: "I hope you do too") is echoed in her outburst to her mother: "I never want to see you again, even in your grave, and I hope you do die." Cromwell bitterly parodies the emotionalism of his earlier films with close-up over-the-shoulder shots of Stanley during her frequent embraces.

For instance, on her first date her thoughts are preoccupied with fantasies of Hollywood and stardom on the one hand, and with demands for boys to treat her as an equal on the other. The latter desire is probably prompted more by her feelings of social inferiority (her quizzing a "nice" boy about what "commoner" pals said about her), brought about by her mother's sudden calling to the Seventh Day Adventist fold. Her mother has occupied the first chapter entitled "Portrait of a Young Girl: Maryland 1930"; the opening shot of the townsfolk brilliantly captures the sagging, lethargic hopelessness of people who are beyond despair in the time of the Depression; their arid, weather-beaten faces mirror the hot, dusty town which offers no hope to its inhabitants. In her Blanche Du Bois style neuroticism, she sees having a good time as the only avenue of escape; the town and her relative's home is a dumping ground for her unwanted child. Her boredom with small towns echoes that of Mary Todd in *Abe Lincoln in Illinois*, but unlike Mary she does not escape, thus her religious conversion (perhaps more fully explained in the uncut version) comes as something of a shock. The inversion of her character, plus the revelation that her daughter overhears as a small child, suggesting that her parentage is uncertain, has driven the child into a lonely existence with her only companion being a cat with whom she feels an empathy.

Twelve years later, with the passing of the New Deal and America's involvement in the Second World War, the child's movement toward fantasy is quite understandable for her love represents a passion for respectability. When she meets the drunken son of a movie producer, it seems her route to a golden opportunity. His suicidal nature provides a common bond of loneliness since he sees love as a means of rejecting his horror and self-pity. With her second husband, Dutch (Lloyd Bridges), her embraces represent fantasy taking over completely; the marriage is a failure as she is set on making a name for herself without considering his feelings. Her constant need for reassurance seems to be awakened only after confrontations between them; she has still not shaken off her feeling of loneliness but she cannot yet afford to shed his name, since as a former sports star, it carries some nostalgic value which is of use to her career. Thus she verbalises her feelings during these embraces as "Do you love me, Dutch?" instead of the earlier, dreamy "I'm going to Hollywood someday." The encounter with the casting-couch studio boss finishes her marriage with a stinging line of irony: "Shall I dress for dinner, or is it informal?"

Author Paddy Chayefsky (right) listens as Cromwell instructs Kim Stanley while a take is set up for THE GODDESS

A star has been born, and the third chapter opens with a pan around a room of trophies and awards. The conversation that takes place is familiar; she is talking of her recent breakdown as her producer is confiding in anybody that will listen that she needs a psychiatrist. Cromwell's observation of the situations, which are normally *clichés* in the run of films about stardom in Hollywood, are governed by a rhythm in the editing and playing which suggest the cyclic tangle in which the characters are inextricably involved: the star finds God through her mother, but rejects her. Not unexpectedly, Cromwell begins the circle moving again with the final segment some five years later, opening with Stanley's breakdown at her mother's funeral. She is now a broken woman, lacking purpose or direction, being guided in a sado-masochistic relationship by her secretary; in one of her few clear moments of vision she accepts the wisdom of her first husband's decision not to let her see their child with the ironic words: "People like us can only love our children."

Cromwell's heroine is both victim and monster; she is allowed an ambiguity of character which many of his villainesses share, but he shows no pity or mercy for the mechanics of the film industry whom he indicts for her downfall. The film offers him an opportunity to vent his love/hate relationship for a lifetime in the industry. He worked subsequently on two other projects filmed outside America, but fought a losing battle with impossible scripts. So he returned to the stage where he has remained active into his eighties. A gentleman of tall bearing, dignified by his snow white hair and moustache, with a congenial nature, whose constant hand movements during conversation betray a restless energy, he is now resident in New York, with his second wife, actress Ruth Nelson, and has recently completed an autobiography.

His Hollywood died with the demise of the old Hollywood

studios. He has worked within the studio system and as an independent with great producers like Selznick, entering the profession as a specialist and assimilating the techniques of making films within a rigid system, but also widening the range of his talent by convincing the studios to accept his projects of broader characterisation at the expense of rigid plot lines and conventional action cliches which in turn gave greater scope to his casts. In spite of the compromises, or perhaps because of them, he has emerged as a highly polished, competent, professional film-maker whose elegant, stylish love stories not only fulfilled the demands of escapist entertainment but were frequently capable of reaching beyond this requirement to add a touch of anti-romantic reality, giving his work a greater durability and plausibility than that of many of his contemporaries.

Acknowledgments

Peter Cowie for making this study possible; Kevin Gough-Yates and Jeremy Boulton of the National Film Archive for arranging screenings; Brenda Davies for her aid and encouragement, and that of all her staff in the British Film Institute Information Library; my wife, Jean, for her aid in preparing the manuscript, and especially John Cromwell for his patience, assistance and for providing stills.

Also Sheila Whitaker of the National Film Archive and Susan Dalton of the State Historical Society of Wisconsin for providing stills, and "Action" magazine for permission to quote from a Leonard Maltin interview with Cromwell, as well as Jack Robins for giving me the time.

JOHN CROMWELL Filmography

As an actor:

THE DUMMY (1929, Robert Milton), playing Walter Babbing.

THE DANCE OF LIFE (1929, Edward Sutherland, John Cromwell), playing a doorkeeper.

THE MIGHTY (1929, John Cromwell), playing Mr. Jamieson.

STREET OF CHANCE (1930, John Cromwell), playing Imbrie.

ABE LINCOLN IN ILLINOIS (G. B: SPIRIT OF THE PEOPLE) (1940, John Cromwell), playing John Brown.

TOP SECRET AFFAIR (G. B.: THEIR SECRET AFFAIR) (1957, H. C. Potter), playing General Grimshaw.

As director:

CLOSE HARMONY (1929). Romance, with a jazz-band background. *Co-dir:* A. Edward Sutherland. *Sc:* Percy Heath (a story by Elsie Janis, Gene Markey). *Dial:* John F. A. Weaver, Percy Heath. *Ph:* J. Roy Hunt. *Ed:* Tay Malarkey. *Songs:* Leo Robin, Richard Whiting, Euday L. Bowman. *With* Charles "Buddy" Rogers (*Al West*), Nancy Carroll (*Marjorie Merwin*), Jack Oakie (*Ben Barney*), Richard "Skeets" Gallagher (*Johnny Bay*), Harry Green (*Max Mindil*), Baby Mack (*Genevieve*), Oscar Smith (*George Washington Brown*), Wade Boteler (*Kelly the cop*), Greta Grandstedt (*Eva Larne*), Gus Partos (*Gustav*), Ricca Allen, Matty Roubert, Jesse Stafford and his Orchestra. *Prod:* for Paramount-Famous Lasky. 6,271 ft.

THE DANCE OF LIFE (1929). Comedy, with a show-business background. *Sc:* Benjamin Glazer (play "Burlesque" by George Manker Watters, Arthur Hopkins). *Dial:* George Manker Watters. *Ph:* J. Roy Hunt. *Ed:* George Nichols Jr. *Titles:* Julian Johnson. *Songs:* Leo Robin, Sam Coslow, Richard Whiting. *Lighting:* Earl Miller. *With* Hal Skelly (*Ralph "Skid" Johnson*), Nancy Carroll (*Bonny Lee King/Bonny Kaye*), Dorothy Revier (*Sylvia Marco*), Ralph Theador (*Harvey Howell*), Charles D. Brown (*Lefty*), Oscar Levant (*Jerry*), Gladys DuBois (*Miss Sherman*), James T. Quinn (*Jimmy*), George Irving (*Minister*), Thelma McNeal ("*Lady of India*"), Gordona Bennett, Miss La Reno, Cora Beach Shumway, Charlotte Ogden, Kay Deslys, Magda Blom (*Amazon Chorus Girls*), John Cromwell (*Doorkeeper*), A. Edward Sutherland (*Theatre Attendant*), Al St. John, James Farley. *Prod:* David O. Selznick for Paramount-Famous Lasky. 10,619 ft. (part sound); 7,488 ft. (silent). Released with Technicolor sequences. A. Edward Sutherland worked as supervising director. Re-made as *When My Baby Smiles At Me* (1948, Walter Lang). Another version of this film was released under the title, *Swing High, Swing Low* (1937, Mitchell Leisen).

THE MIGHTY (1929). The dramatic story of the regeneration of a crook on the battlefield. *Sc:* Grover Jones, William Slavens McNutt, Nellie Reville (a story by Robert N. Lee). *Add. dial:* Grover Jones, William Slavens McNutt. *Ph:* J. Roy Hunt. *Ed:* George Nicholls Jr., Otto Lovering. *With* George Bancroft (*Blake Greeson*), Esther Ralston (*Louise Patter-*

son), Warner Oland ("Shiv" Sterky), Raymond Hatton (Dogey Frank), Dorothy Revier (Mayme), Morgan Farley (Jerry Patterson), O. P. Heggie, Charles Sellon, E. H. Calvert, John Cromwell. Prod: Paramount-Famous Lasky. 6,802 ft.

THE STREET OF CHANCE (1930). A gambler sacrifices his life to save his young brother from following him into the profession. Sc: Howard Estabrook (a story by Oliver H. P. Garrett). Dial: Lenore Coffee. Ph: Charles Lang. Ed: Otto Lovering. Titles: Gerald Geraghty. With William Powell ("Natural" Davis/ J. B. Marsden), Kay Francis (Alma), Jean Arthur (Judith Marsden), Regis Toomey ("Babe" Marsden), Stanley Fields (Dorgan), Brooks Benedict, Betty Francisco, Joan Standing, John Risso, Maurice Black, Irving Bacon, John Cromwell. Prod: David O. Selznick for Paramount-Famous Lasky. 7,023 ft. 76 mins. Re-made in 1937 as Her Husband Lies (dir: Edward Ludwig).

THE TEXAN (1930). A young outlaw impersonates a Spanish lady's dead son in order to rob her, but has a change of heart and protects her life and property. Sc: Oliver H. P. Garrett, Daniel Rubin (a story, "A Double-Dyed Deceiver" by O. Henry). Dial: Daniel Rubin. Ph: Victor Milner. Ed: Verna Willis. Songs: L. Wolfe Gilbert, Abel Baer. With Gary Cooper (Enrique "Quico"/The Llano Kid), Fay Wray (Consuela), Emma Dunn (Senora Ibarra), Oscar Apfel (Thacker), James Marcus (John Brown), Soledad Jiminez, Donald Reed, Edward Brady, Romualdo Tirado, Enrique Acosta, Cesas Vanoni, Veda Buckland. Prod: David O. Selznick for Paramount-Publix. 72m.

SEVEN DAYS LEAVE (GB: MEDALS) (1930). An old lady invents a son so that she can feel she played her part in the First World War, but then a man whose name she has used arrives on her doorstep. Co-dir: Richard Wallace. Sc: John Farrow, Don Totheroh (a play "The Old Lady Shows Her Medals" by Sir James Barrie). Ph: Charles Lang. Ed: George Nicholls Jr. Art dir: Bernard Herzbrun. Music: Frank Terry. Titles: Richard Digges Jr. With Gary Cooper (Kenneth Dowey), Beryl Mercer (Sarah Ann Dowey), Daisy Belmore (Emma Mickelham), Nora Cecil (Amelia Twymley), Tempe Pigott (Mrs. Haggerty), Arthur Hoyt, Arthur Metcalfe, Basil Radford. Prod: Louis D. Lighton for Paramount-Famous Lasky. 80m. Cromwell disputes this credit, claiming he was hired to work on dialogue scenes, and in fact contributed nothing to the finished film.

FOR THE DEFENSE (1930). A successful shyster lawyer runs into trouble when he tries to cover up for a crime committed by his fiancée. Sc: Oliver H. P. Garrett (a story by Jules Furthman). Ph: Charles Lang. Ed: George Nicholls Jr. With William Powell (William Foster), Kay Francis (Irene Manners), Scott Kolk (Defoe), William B. Davidson (District Attorney Stone), John Elliott (McGann), Thomas E. Jackson (Daly), Harry Walker, James Finlayson, Charles West, Charles Sullivan, Ernest S. Adams, Bertram Marbaugh, Edward Le Saint, John Cromwell. Prod: Paramount-Publix. 65m.

TOM SAWYER (1930). The second film version of Mark Twain's novel about a youngster and his life on the Mississippi. *Sc:* Sam Mintz, Grover Jones, William Slavens McNutt (a novel "The Adventures of Tom Sawyer" by Mark Twain). *Ph:* Charles Lang. *Ed:* Alyson Shaffer. *Art dir:* Bernard Herzbrun, Robert O'Dell. *With* Jackie Coogan (*Tom Sawyer*), Junior Durkin (*Huck Finn*), Lucien Littlefield (*The Teacher*), Tully Marshall (*Muff Potter*), Clara Blandick (*Aunt Polly*), Mitzi Green, Lon Puff, Ethel Wales, Mary Jane Irving, Jackie Searl, Charles Stevens, Dick Winslow, Jane Darwell, Charles Sellon. *Prod:* Louis D. Lighton for Paramount-Publix. 85m. Other versions include *The Adventures of Tom Sawyer* (1917, William D. Taylor); *The Adventures of Tom Sawyer* (1937, Norman Taurog); *The Adventures of Tom Sawyer* (1969, Mihai Jacob, a Rumanian-French co-production); *Tom Sawyer* (1973, Don Taylor, a musical version); *Tom Sawyer* (1973, James Neilson, TV feature shown theatrically).

SCANDAL SHEET (1931). Drama about a scandal sheet editor finding out the facts about a man with whom his wife intends to elope. *Sc:* Vincent Lawrence, Max Marcin (a story by Oliver H. P. Garrett). *Ph:* David Abel. *Ed:* George Nicholls Jr. *With* George Bancroft (*Mark Flint*), Kay Francis (*Edith Flint*), Clive Brook (*Noel Adams*), Regis Toomey (*Regan*), Lucien Littlefield (*McCloskey*), Gilbert Emery, Mary Foy, Jackie Searl, James Kelsey, Harry Beresford. *Prod:* Paramount-Publix. 77m.

UNFAITHFUL (1931). A woman sacrifices her good name to save her brother from being disillusioned by his wife's unfaithfulness. *Sc.* Eve Unsell (story by John Van Druten). *Add. dial:* John Van Druten. *Ph:* Charles Lang. *With* Ruth Chatterton (*Fay, Viscountess Kilkerry*), Paul Lukas (*Karl Heidon*), Paul Cavanaugh (*Ronald, Viscount Kilkerry*), Juliette Compton (*Gemina Houston*), Donald Cook (*Terry Houston*), Sid Saylor, Emily Fitzroy, Bruce Warren, Arnold Lucy, Leslie Palmer, Dennis D'Auborn, Ambrose Barker, Stella Moore, Capt. George Jackson, Eric Kalhurt, Douglas Gilmore, Jack Richardson. *Prod:* Paramount-Publix. 70m.

VICE SQUAD (1931). The vice squad trick a foreign emissary into squealing on an infamous gang of crooks. *Sc:* Oliver H. P. Garrett. *Ph:* Charles Lang. *With* Paul Lukas (*Stephen Lucarno*), Kay Francis (*Alice Morrison*), Helen Johnson (*Madeline Hunt*), William B. Davidson (*Magistrate Morrison*), Rockliffe Fellowes (*Det-Sgt. Mather*), Esther Howard, Monte Carter, G. Pat Collins, Phil Tead, Davison Clark, Tom Wilson, James Durkin, William Arnold. *Prod:* Paramount-Publix. 80m.

RICH MAN'S FOLLY (1931). A film version of one of Dickens's lesser known novels. *Sc:* Grover Jones, Edward Paramore Jr. (novel "Dombey and Son" by Charles Dickens). *Ph:* David Abel. *With* George Bancroft (*Brock Trumbull*), Frances Dee (*Ann Trumbull*), Robert Ames (*Joseph Warren*), Juliette Compton (*Paula Norcross*), David Durand (*Brock Trumbull Jr.*), Dorothy Peterson, Harry Allen, Dawn O'Day, Gilbert Emery, Guy Oliver, George McFarlane, William Arnold. *Prod:* Louis D. Lighton for Paramount-Publix. 80m. Previous version as *Dombey and Son* (1917, Maurice Elvey).

THE WORLD AND THE FLESH (1932). A soldier of fortune risks his life

George Bancroft, Miriam Hopkins (centre) and player in
THE WORLD AND THE FLESH

to save a rich girl's friends during the Russian Revolution—at a price! *Sc:* Oliver H. P. Garrett (a play by Philip Zaska, Ernst Stitz). *Ph:* Karl Struss. *With* George Bancroft (*Kylenko*), Miriam Hopkins (*Maria Yaskaya*), Alan Mowbray (*Dmitri*), George E. Stone (*Rutchkin*), Emmett Corrigan (*General Spiro*), Max Wagner, Mitchell Lewis, Harry Cording, Reginald Barlow, Oscar Apfel, Ferike Boros. *Prod:* Paramount-Publix Corp. 75m.

SWEEPINGS (1933). The disappointments and disillusion of a man whose family fail to live up to his expectations. *Sc:* Lester Cohen, Howard Estabrook, H. W. Havemann (a novel by Lester Cohen). *Ph:* Edward Cronjager. *Ed:* George Nicholls Jr. *Music:* Max Steiner. *With* Lionel Barrymore (*Daniel Pardway*), Alan Dinehart (*Thane Pardway*), Eric Linden (*Freddie Pardway*), William Gargan (*Gene Pardway*), Gloria Stuart (*Phoebe Pardway*), Gregory Ratoff, Lucien Littlefield, Ninetta Sunderland, Helen Mack, George Meeker, Ivan Lebedeff. *Prod:* David O. Selznick for RKO. 80m.

THE SILVER CORD (1933). A young girl rebels against the strictures of her interfering mother-in-law. *Sc:* Jane Murfin (a play by Sidney Howard). *Ph:* Charles Rosher. *Ed:* George Nicholls Jr. *Music:* Max Steiner. *With* Irene Dunne (*Christina Phelps*), Joel McCrea (*David Phelps*), Frances Dee (*Hester Phelps*), Laura Hope Crews (*Mrs. Phelps*), Eric Linden (*Robert Phelps*), Helen Cromwell. *Prod:* RKO. 75m.

DOUBLE HARNESS (1933). Comedy, with a society girl tricking a bachelor into marriage and cementing their relationship by guiding his interest from frivolity into the world of big business. *Sc:* Jane Murfin (a play by Edward P. Montgomery). *Ph:* J. Roy Hunt. *Ed:* George

Nicholls Jr. *Music:* Max Steiner. *With* Ann Harding (*Joan Colby*), William Powell (*John Fletcher*), Henry Stephenson (*Col. Colby*), Lilian Bond (*Monica*), George Meeker (*Dennis*), Reginald Owen, Kay Hammond, Lucille Browne, Leigh Allen, Hugh Huntley, Wallis Clark, Fred Santley. *Prod:* RKO. 70m.

ANN VICKERS (1933). A mirror image of *Caged;* the story of a female social worker exposing terrible prison conditions. *Sc:* Jane Murfin (the novel by Sinclair Lewis). *Ph:* David Abel. *Art dir:* Van Nest Polglase, Charles Kirk. *Ed:* George Nicholls Jr. *Music:* Max Steiner. *With* Irene Dunne (*Ann Vickers*), Walter

Irene Dunne and Helen Eby Rock in ANN VICKERS

Huston (*Barney Dolphin*), Conrad Nagel (*Lindsey Atwell*), Bruce Cabot (*Captain Resnick*), Edna May Oliver (*Malvona Wormser*), Sam Hardy, Ferdinand Gottschalk, Raefaela Ottiano, Mitchell Lewis, Helen Eby-Rock, Gertrude Michael, Murray Kinnell. *Prod:* Pandro S. Berman, Merian C. Cooper for RKO. 69m.

SPITFIRE (1934). Title refers to the temperament of a hill-billy girl with two suitors, one of whom is married. *Sc:* Jane Murfin, Lula Vollmer (a play "Trigger" by Lula Vollmer). *Ph:* Edward Cronjager. *Art dir:* Van Nest Polglase, Carroll Clark. *Ed:* George Nicholls Jr. *Music:* Max Steiner. *With* Katharine

Hepburn (*Trigger Hicks*), Robert Young (*John Stafford*), Ralph Bellamy (*Fleetwood*), Martha Sleeper (*Eleanore Stafford*), Louis Mason (*Grayson*), Sara Haden, High Ghere, Virginio Howell, Therese Wittler, Sidney Toler, John Beck. *Assoc. prod:* Pandro S. Berman. *Prod:* Merian C. Cooper for RKO. 88m.

THIS MAN IS MINE (1934). Romantic comedy-drama with patient wife winning back philandering husband from seductress. *Sc:* Jane Murfin (a story by Anne Morrison Chapin). *Ph:* David Abel. *Art dir:* Van Nest Polglase, Carroll Clark. *Ed:* William Morgan. *Music:* Max Steiner. *With* Irene Dunne (*Tony Dunlap*), Con-

Irene Dunne and Ralph Bellamy in THIS MAN IS MINE

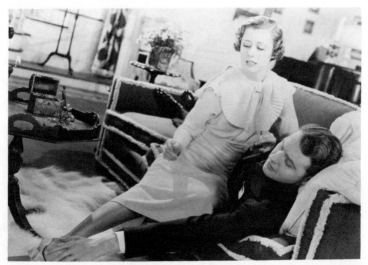

stance Cummings (*Fran Harper*), Ralph Bellamy (*Jim Dunlap*), Kay Johnson (*Bee McCrea*), Charles Starrett (*Jud McCrea*), Sidney Blackmer, Louis Mason. *Prod:* RKO. 76m.

OF HUMAN BONDAGE (1934). One of Bette Davis's first important roles as a slatternly waitress who enslaves a naïve medical student. *Sc:* Lester Cohen (a novel by Somerset Maugham). *Ph:* Henry W. Gerrard. *Art dir:* Van Nest Polglase, Carroll Clark. *Ed:* William Morgan. *Music:* Max Steiner. *With* Bette Davis (*Mildred*), Leslie Howard (*Philip Carey*), Frances Dee (*Sally*), Kay Johnson (*Nora*), Reginald Denny (*Griffiths*), Alan Hale (*Muller*), Reginald Owen, Reginald Sheffield, Desmond Roberts. *Prod:* Pandro S. Berman for RKO. 83m. Re-made by Edmund Goulding in 1946, and by Ken Hughes (and Henry Hathaway and Bryan Forbes) in 1964.

THE FOUNTAIN (1934). Romantic drama with an exiled Englishwoman living in Holland during the First World War, who has to tell her wounded German husband that she has fallen in love with an interned British flier [and childhood friend]. *Sc:* Jane Murfin (a novel by Charles Morgan). *Add. dial:* Sam Hoffenstein. *Ph:* Henry W. Gerrard. *Art dir:* Van Nest Polglase, Carroll Clark. *Ed:* William Morgan. *Music:* Max Steiner. *With* Ann Harding (*Julie*), Paul Lukas (*Rupert*), Brian Aherne (*Lewis Alison*), Jean Hersholt (*Baron Van Leyden*), Ralph Forbes (*Ballater*), Violet Kemble Cooper (*Baroness Van Leyden*), Sara Haden, Betty Alden, Richard Abbott, Barbara Barondess, Douglas Wood, Ian Wolfe, Frank Reicher, Ferike Boros, Christian Rub, William Stack, Charles McNaugh-

ton, Desmond Roberts, J. M. Kerrigan, Rudolph Amendt. *Prod:* Pandro S. Berman for RKO. 83m.

VILLAGE TALE (1935). One of Cromwell's favourite projects: about a small town and its dramas, which he described as a series of character studies rather than a plot. *Sc:* Allan Scott (a novel by Phil Stong). *Ph:* Nicholas Musuraca. *Art dir:* Van Nest Polglase, Carroll Clark. *Ed:* William Morgan. *Music:* Al Colombo. *With* Randolph Scott (*Slaughter Somerville*), Kay Johnson (*Janet Stevenson*), Guinn "Big Boy" Williams (*Ben Roberts*), Arthur Hohl (*Elmer Stevenson*), Robert Barrat (*Drury Stevenson*), Janet Beecher (*Amy Somerville*), Edward El-

Guinn 'Big Boy' Williams and Ann Dvorak in VILLAGE TALE

lis, Dorothy Burgess, Andy Clyde, Ray Mayer, T. Roy Barnes, DeWitt Jennings, Donald Meek. *Prod:* David Hempstead for RKO. 80m.

JALNA (1935). Another familiar saga, based on the work of a popular novelist. *Sc:* Anthony Veiller (a novel by Mazo de la Roche). *Adap:* Garrett Fort, Larry Bachman. *Ph:* Edward Cronjager. *Art dir:* Van Nest Polglase, Charles Kirk. *Ed:* William Morgan. *Music:* Al Colombo. *With* Kay Johnson (*Alayne*), Ian Hunter (*Renny*), C. Aubrey Smith (*Nicholas*), Nigel Bruce (*Maurice*), David Manners (*Eden*), Peggy Wood (*Meg*), Jessie Ralph, Theodore Newton, George Offerman Jr., Halliwell Hobbes, Clifford Severn, Molly Lamont, Forrester Harvey. *Prod:* Kenneth Macgowan for RKO. 77m.

I DREAM TOO MUCH (1935). Opera star Lily Pons weds music student Henry Fonda, but their marriage runs into trouble over their respective career interests. *Sc:* James Gow, Edmund North (a story by Elsie Finn, David G. Wittels). *Ph:* David Abel. *Art dir:* Van Nest Polglase, Charles Kirk. *Ed:* William Morgan. *Music:* Jerome Kern, Dorothy Fields. *Operatic conductor:* Andre Kostelanetz. *Dance dir:* Hermes Pan. *With* Henry Fonda (*Jonathan*), Lily Pons (*Annette*), Eric Blore (*Roger*), Osgood Perkins (*Darcy*), Lucille Ball (*Gwendolyn Dilley*), Mischa Auer (*Pianist*), Lucien Littlefield, Paul Porcasi, Scotty Beckett, Esther Dale. *Prod:* Pandro S. Berman for RKO. 95m.

LITTLE LORD FAUNTLEROY (1936). A nice little boy becomes heir to a fortune, wins over his craggy grandfather, breaking down the latter's prejudices, and is restored to his rightful position when his American friends foil a false claimant to the title. *Sc:* Hugh Walpole (the play by Frances Hodgson Burnett). *Ph:* Charles Rosher. *Art dir:* Sturges Carne. *Ed:* Harold Kern. *Music:* Max Steiner. *With* Freddie Bartholomew (*Ceddie*), Dolores Costello (*"Dearest"*), Sir C. Aubrey Smith (*The Earl of Dorincourt*), Guy Kibbee (*Mr. Hobbs*), Mickey Rooney (*Dick*), Henry Stephenson (*Havisham*), Jessie Ralph, Jackie Searl, Helen Flint, Una O'Connor, E. E. Clive, Ivan Simpson, Constance Collier, Eric Alden, May Beatty, Virginia Field, Reginald Barlow, Lionel Belmore, Tempe Pigott, Gilbert Emery, Lawrence Grant, Walter Kingsford, Eily Malyon, Fred Walton, Robert Emmett O'Connor, Elsa Buchanan, John Standing, Joseph Tyzack, Alex Pollard, Daisy Belmore, "Prince." *Prod:* David O. Selznick for United Artists. Earlier versions in 1922 directed by A. E. Green, Jack Pickford; 1914, directed by F. Martin Thornton (G.B.).

TO MARY—WITH LOVE (1936). Another marital drama; Claire Trevor tries to come between Warner Baxter and Myrna Loy, but all ends happily. *Sc:* Richard Sherman, Howard Ellis Smith (a story by Richard Sherman). *Ph:* Sidney Wagner. *Art dir:* Mark-Lee Kirk. *Ed:* Ralph Dietrich. *Music:* Louis Silvers. *With* Warner Baxter (*Jack Wallace*), Myrna Loy (*Mary Wallace*), Claire Trevor (*Kitty Brant*), Ian Hunter (*Bill Hallam*), Jean Dixon (*Irene*), Pat Somerset (*Sloan Potter*), Helen Brown, Harold Forshay, Wedgewood Nowell, Paul Hurst, Franklin Pangborn, Tyler Brooke, Arthur Aylesworth, Edward Cooper, Florence Lake, Margaret Fielding, Ruth Clifford. *Assoc. Prod:* Kenneth Macgowan. *Prod:* Darryl F. Zanuck for 20th Century-Fox. 87m.

BANJO ON MY KNEE (1936). Riverboat gal Barbara Stanwyck sings, dances and fights her way to the arms of Joel McCrea with the aid of a good supporting cast. *Sc:* Nunnally Johnson (a novel by Harry Hamilton). *Ph:* Ernest Palmer. *Art dir:* none credited. *Ed:* Hansen Fritsch. *Music:* Arthur Lange. *With* Barbara Stanwyck (*Pearl*), Joel McCrea (*Ernie*), Buddy Ebsen (*Buddy*), Walter Brennan (*Newt Holley*), Helen Westley (*Grandma*), Walter Catlett (*Warfield Scott*), Anthony Martin, Katherine De Mille, Victor Kilian, George Humbert, Hilda Vaughn, Cecil Weston, Louis Mason, The Hall Johnson Choir. *Assoc. prod:*

Nunnally Johnson. *Prod:* Darryl F. Zanuck for 20th Century-Fox. 80m.

THE PRISONER OF ZENDA (1937). Ruritanian melodrama with an Englishman impersonating a look-alike king, falling for his Queen, and eliminating one of the King's main enemies. *Sc:* John Balderston, Wells Root (a novel by Anthony Hope). *Add. dial:* Donald Ogden Stewart. *Ph:* James Wong Howe. *Art dir:* Lyle Wheeler. *Ed:* Harold Kern. *Music:* Alfred Newman. *With* Ronald Colman (*Rudolf Rassendyll/King Rudolf V*), Madeleine Carroll (*Princess Flavia*), Raymond Massey (*Black Michael*), Douglas Fairbanks (*Rupert of Hentzau*), Mary Astor (*Antoinette de Mauban*), David Niven (*Fritz von Tarlenheim*),

Left, Douglas Fairbanks Jr. and Ronald Colman duel in THE PRISONER OF ZENDA. Right, John Cromwell works out an idea with a viewfinder during the film's production, watched left by cinematographer James Wong Howe

Sir C. Aubrey Smith (*Colonel Zapt*), Lawrence Grant, Ian MacLaren, Howard Lang, Byron Foulger, Ralph Faulkner, Montagu Love, William von Brincken, Philip Sleeman, Ben Webster, Alexander D'Arcy, Evelyn Beresford, Emmett King, Boyd Irwin, Al Sheen, Charles Halton, Spencer Charters, Eleanor Wesselhoeft, Henry Roquemore, Pat Somerset, Lillian Harmer, Leslie Sketchley, Florence Roberts, Torben Meyer, Otto Fries. *Prod:* David O. Selznick for United Artists. *Assoc. prod:* William H. Wright. 101m. Additional direction by George Cukor and Woody Van Dyke uncredited. Other versions in 1915 (George Loane Tucker); 1922 (Rex Ingram); 1952 (Richard Thorpe).

ALGIERS (1938). Re-make of a French success, with romance getting the better of a charming criminal's judgement, during a battle of wits with a police chief who is trying to lure him out of the Casbah. *Sc:* John Howard Lawson (from the screenplay by Julien Duvivier, Roger Ashelbe for *Pepe Le Moko* [1936]). *Add. dial:* James M. Cain. *Ph:* James Wong Howe. *Art dir:* Alexander Tulahoff. *Ed:* None credited. *Music:* Vincent Scotto, Mohammed Igorbouchen. *With* Charles Boyer (*Pepe Le Moko*), Hedy Lamarr (*Gaby*), Sigrid Gurie (*Ines*), Joseph Calleia (*Slimane*), Alan Hale (*Grand Pere*), Gene Lockhart (*Regis*), Johnny Downs, Stanley Fields, Robert Greig, Nina Koshetz, Joan Woodbury, Claudia Dell, Charles D. Brown, Ben Hall, Armand Kaliz, Walter Kingsford, Paul Harvey, Bert Roach, Luana Walters. *Prod:* Walter Wanger for United Artists. 95m. Re-make of *Pepe Le Moko* (1936, Julien Duvivier); re-made as *Casbah*

(1948, John Berry).

MADE FOR EACH OTHER (1939). Newly-wed couple prove the truth of the title by sticking together through every trial and tribulation in a heartwarming romantic drama. *Sc:* Jo Swerling. *Ph:* Leon Shamroy. *Art dir:* Lyle Wheeler. *Ed:* Harold Kern, James Newcomb. *Music:* Lou Forbes. *Interior decor:* Edward Boyle. *With* Carole Lombard (*Jane Mason*), James Stewart (*John Mason*), Charles Coburn (*Judge Doolittle*), Lucile Watson (*Mrs. Mason*), Eddie Quillan, Alma Kruger, Ruth Weston, Donald Briggs, Harry Davenport, Esther Dale, Ward Bond, Renee Orsell, Louise Beavers, Olin Howland, Fern Emmett, Jackie Taylor, Mickey Rentschler, Ivan Simpson, Russell Hopton, Bonnie Belle Barber. *Prod:* David O. Selznick for United Artists. 90m. [U.S.A.]; 85m. [G.B.].

IN NAME ONLY (1939). Romantic melodrama; a selfish socialite wife who refuses to divorce Cary Grant, is the only obstacle standing in the way of his love for Carole Lombard. *Sc:* Richard Sherman (a novel by Bessie Breuer). *Ph:* J. Roy Hunt. *Art dir:* Van Nest Polglase, Perry Ferguson. *Ed:* William Hamilton. *Music:* Roy Webb. *With* Carole Lombard (*Julie Eden*), Cary Grant (*Alec Walker*), Kay Francis (*Maida Walker*), Charles Coburn (*Mr. Walker*), Jonathan Hale (*Dr. Gateson*), Nella Walker (*Mrs. Walker*), Katherine Alexander, Spencer Charters, Peggy Ann Garner, Helen Vinson, Maurice Moscovitch. *Prod:* George Haight. *Exec. prod:* Pandro S. Berman for RKO. 92m. Shooting started under the title of the original novel, "Memory of Love"; this was also a stock title for

125

other RKO projects including Cromwell's *Night Song* (1947), and it is often incorrectly listed as a separate Cromwell film. Further confusion arose with the 1949 release of a Swedish-American production of this name, but Cromwell definitely did not work on that one.

ABE LINCOLN IN ILLINOIS (G.B: SPIRIT OF THE PEOPLE) (1940). A dramatisation of Lincoln's early days as a lawyer, and his marriage to Mary Todd Lincoln who is determined, against all odds, to push him forward in his career.

Sc: Robert E. Sherwood, Grover Jones (a play by Robert E. Sherwood). *Ph:* James Wong Howe. *Art dir:* Van Nest Polglase. *Ed:* George Hively. *Music:* Roy Webb. *Montage:* Douglas Travers. *With* Raymond Massey (*Abe Lincoln*), Ruth Gordon (*Mary Todd Lincoln*), Gene Lockhart (*Stephen Douglas*), May Howard (*Ann Rutledge*), Dorothy Tree (*Elizabeth Edwards*), Harvey Stephens (*Ninian Edwards*), Minor Watson, Alan Baxter, Louis Jean Heydt, Howard Da Silva, Aldrich Bowker, Clem Bevans,

Glenn Ford, player, and Margaret Sullavan in
SO ENDS OUR NIGHT

Maurice Murphy, Fay Helm, Harlan Briggs, Herbert Rudley, Andy Clyde, Roger Imhof, Florence Roberts, Leona Roberts, Edmund Elton, Syd Saylor, George Rosener, Trevor Bardette, Charles Middleton, Elizabeth Risdon, Napoleon Simpson, Alec Craig, John Cromwell. *Prod:* Max Gordon for RKO. 110m.

VICTORY (1940). A band of cut-throats threaten the idyllic life of an island's inhabitants in this lush version of Joseph Conrad's novel. *Sc:* John L. Balderston (the novel by Joseph Conrad). *Ph:* Leo Tover. *Art dir:* Hans Dreier, Robert Usher. *Ed:* William Shea. *Music:* Frederick Hollander. *With* Fredric March (*Hendrik Heyst*), Betty Field (*Alma*), Sir Cedric Hardwicke (*Narrator*), Sig Ruman (*Schomberg*), Margaret Wycherly (*Mrs. Schomberg*), Fritz Feld (*Makanoff*), Jerome Cowan, Rafaela Ottiano, Lionel Royce, Chester Gan. *Prod:* Anthony Veiller for Paramount. 78m. Other versions include *Victory* (1919, Maurice Tourneur) and *Dangerous Paradise* (1930, William A. Wellman).

SO ENDS OUR NIGHT (1941). Vivid version of the Remarque novel, with Fredric March rejecting the Nazi *régime*, and fleeing the country with the villains in pursuit. *Sc:* Talbot Jennings (novel "Flotsam" by Erich Maria Remarque). *Ph:* William Daniels. *Art dir:* Jack Otterson. *Ed:* William Reynolds. *Music:* Louis Gruenberg. *With* Fredric March (*Josef Steiner*), Margaret Sullavan (*Ruth Holland*), Frances Dee (*Marie Steiner*), Glenn Ford (*Ludwig Kern*), Anna Sten (*Lilo*), Érich von Stroheim (*Brenner*), Allan Brett, Joseph Cawthorne, Leonid Kinskey, Sig Ruman, Alexander Granach, Roman Bohnen, William Stack, Lionel Royce, Ernst Deutsch, Joe Marks, Spencer Charters, Hans Schumann, Walter Stahl, Philip van Zandt, Fredrik Vogeding, Gerba Rozen, James Bush, Emory Parnell, Kate McKenna, William van Brincken, Edith Argold, Edward Fielding, Gisela Werbezink. *Prod:* David L. Loew, Albert Lewin for United Artists. 117m.

SON OF FURY (1942). Disinherited by his treacherous uncle, the hero flees to a desert island where he befriends the natives and plots his revenge on the dastardly uncle. *Sc:* Philip Dunne (novel "Benjamin Blake" by Edison Marshall). *Ph:* Arthur Miller. *Art dir:* Richard Day, James Basevi. *Ed:* Walter Thompson. *Music:* Alfred Newman. *With* Tyrone Power (*Benjamin Blake*), Gene Tierney (*Eve*), George Sanders (*Sir Arthur Blake*), Frances Farmer (*Isabel Blake*), John Carradine (*Caleb Green*), Roddy McDowall (*Benjamin, as a boy*), Elsa Lanchester (*Bristol Isabel*), Harry Davenport, Dudley Digges, Halliwell Hobbes, Marten Lamont, Arthur Hohl, Ray Mala, Pedro de Cordoba, Heather Thatcher, Charles Irwin, Lester Matthews, Dennis Hoey, Ethel Griffies, Robert Greig, Clifford Severn. *Prod:* Darryl F. Zanuck for 20th Century-Fox. *Assoc. prod:* William Perlberg. 98m. Re-made as *Treasure of the Golden Condor* (1952, Delmer Daves).

SINCE YOU WENT AWAY (1944). Ambitious Selznick project about the problems of an American family during the Second World War. *Sc:* David O. Selznick. *Ph:* Lee Garmes, Stanley Cortez. *Prod. designer:* William L. Pereira. *Sets:* Mark-Lee Kirk. *Ed:* Harold Kern. *Music:* Max Steiner. *Dance dir:* Charles Walters. *With* Claudette Colbert (*Anne Hilton*),

Jennifer Jones (*Jane*), Shirley Temple (*Bridget*), Joseph Cotten (*Lt. Anthony Willett, U.S.N.*), Monty Woolley (*Colonel Smollett*), Robert Walker (*Corporal William G. Smollett*), Lionel Barrymore (*Clergyman*), Hattie McDaniel, Agnes Moorehead, Guy Madison, Nazimova, Keenan Wynn, Gordon Oliver, Charles Williams, Lloyd Corrigan, June Devlin, Albert Basserman, Craig Stevens, Neila Hunt, Jackie Moran, Anne Gillis, Robert Anderson, Irving Bacon, Aileen Pringle, Wallis Clark, James Carlisle, Leonide Mostovoy, Dorothy Garner, Joyce Horan, John A. James, Mary Anne Durkin, Richard C. Wood, Ruth Valmy, Grady Sutton, Buddy Gorman, Tom Dawson, Patricia Peters, Andrew McLaglen, Addison Richards, George Lloyd, Barbara Pepper, Florence Bates, Jill Warren, Byron Foulger, Harry Hayden, Edwin Maxwell, Russell Hoyt, Louella Clarr, Helen Koford, Don Marjorian, Conrad Binyon, Theodore von Eltz, Adeline de Walt Reynolds, Jimmy Dodd, Christopher Adams, Martha Outlaw, Verna Knopf, Jonathan Hale, Robert Cherny, Kirk Barron, Earl Jacobs, Cecil Ballerino, Jack Gardner, Doodles Weaver, James Westerfield, Warren Hymer, Ralph Reed, Paul Esberg, William Jillson, Dorothy Mann, Peggy Maley, Robert Johnson, Derek Harris, Dorothy Dandridge, Eddie Hall, Warren Barr, Neyle Marx, Johnny Bond, Ruth Roman, Betsy Howard, Terry Revell, Stephen Wayne, William B. Davidson, Walter Baldwin, Marilyn Hume, Eric Sinclair, Jimmy Clemens Jr., Soda the bulldog. *Prod:* David O. Selznick for United Artists. 171m.

THE ENCHANTED COTTAGE (1945). A sensitively-handled fantasy about two misfits finding love in a New England cottage. *Sc:* DeWitt Bodeen, Herman J. Mankiewicz (a play by Sir Arthur Wing Pinero). *Ph:* Ted Tetzlaff. *Art dir:* Albert D'Agostino, Carroll Clark. *Ed:* Joseph Noreiga. *Music:* Constantin Bakaleinikoff. *With* Dorothy McGuire (*Lanra*), Robert Young (*Oliver*), Herbert Marshall (*Hillgrove*), Mildred Natwick (*Mrs. Minnett*), Spring Byington (*Violet Price*), Richard Gaines (*Frederick*), Hillary Brooke, Alec Englander, Mary Worth, Robert Clarke, Josephine Whittell, Eden Nichols. *Prod:* Harriet Parsons. 92m. *Exec. prod:* Jack J. Gross for RKO. A silent version of *The Enchanted Cottage* was directed in 1924 by John S. Robertson.

ANNA AND THE KING OF SIAM (1946). The first (non-musical) version of the story of the battle of wits between an English governess and a Thailand King. *Sc:* Talbot Jennings, Sally Brown (a novel by Margaret Landon). *Ph:* Arthur Miller. *Art dir:* Lyle R. Wheeler, William Darling. *Ed:* Harmon Jones. *Music:* Bernard Herrman. *With* Rex Harrison (*King Mongkut*), Irene Dunne (*Anna Owens*), Linda Darnell (*Tuptin*), Gale Sondergaard (*Lady Thiang*), Richard Lyon (*Louis Owens*), Lee J. Cobb, Marjorie Eaton, Diana van den Ecker, Mikhail Rasumny, Dennis Hoey, Tito Renaldo, William Edmunds, John Abbott, Connie Leon, Leonard Strong, Mickey Roth, Si-Lan Chan, Helene Grant, Stanley Mann, Addison Richards, Neyle Morrow, Julian Rivero, Chet Voravasi, Jean Wong, Dorothy Chang. *Prod:* Louis D. Lighton for 20th Century-Fox. 128m. Re-made as *The King and I* (1956, Walter Lang).

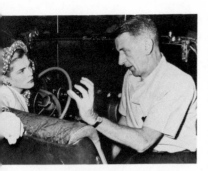

John Cromwell directs Lizabeth
Scott in DEAD RECKONING

DEAD RECKONING (1947). A tough
Second World War veteran becomes em-
broiled in violence when he investigates
the murder of a soldier friend. *Sc:* Oliver
H. P. Garrett, Steve Fisher (a story by
Gerald Drayson Adams, Sidney Biddell,
adapted by Allen Rivkin). *Ph:* Leo Tover.
Art dir: Stephen Goosson, Rudolph Stern-
ard. *Ed:* Gene Havlick. *Music:* Marlin
Skiles. *With* Humphrey Bogart (*Rip
Murdock*), Lizabeth Scott (*Coral Chand-
ler*), Morris Carnovsky (*Martinelli*),
Charles Cane (*Lt. Kincaid*), William
Prince (*Johnny Drake*), Marvin Miller
(*Krause*), Wallace Ford, William For-
rest, James Bell, George Chandler, Ruby
Dandridge. *Prod:* Sidney Biddell for
Columbia. 100m.

NIGHT SONG (1947). Drama revolving
around a socialite falling in love with a
blind pianist. *Sc:* Frank Fenton, Dick
Irving Hyland (a story by Dick Irving
Hyland). *Ph:* Lucien Ballard. *Art dir:*
Albert D'Agostino, Jack Okey. *Ed:* Harry
Marker. *Music:* Leigh Stevens. *With*
Dana Andrews (*Dan*), Merle Oberon
(*Cathy*), Donald Curtis (*George*), Ethel
Barrymore (*Miss Wiley*), Hoagy Car-
michael (*Chick*), Walter Reed, Jacque-
line White, Arthur Rubinstein, Eugene
Ormandy, Jane Jones, Whit Bissell. *Prod:*
Harriet Parsons. *Exec. prod:* Jack J. Gross
for RKO. 101m.

CAGED (1950). A young first offender
is brutalized by a spell in a women's
prison. *Sc:* Virginia Kellogg, Bernard C.
Schoenfeld (their own story), *Ph:* Carl
Guthrie. *Art dir:* Charles Clarke. *Ed:*
Owen Marks. *Music:* Max Steiner. *With*
Eleanor Parker (*Marie Allen*), Agnes
Moorehead (*Ruth Benton*), Hope Emer-
son (*Evelyn Harper*), Betty Garde
(*Kitty*), Lee Patrick (*Elvira Powell*),
Jan Sterling (*Smoochie*), Frances Morris,
Ellen Corby, Olive Deering, Jane Dar-
well, Sheila Stevens, Gertrude Michael,
Joan Miller, Lynn Sherman, Marjorie
Crossland, Taylor Holmes, Don Beddoe,
Moroni Olsen. *Prod:* Jerry Wald for
Warner Bros. 96m.

THE COMPANY SHE KEEPS (1951).
Both sides of the law are involved in a
romantic triangle as a parole officer and
an ex-con vie for the love of Dennis
O'Keefe. *Sc:* Ketti Frings (her own
story). *Ph:* Nicholas Musuraca. *Art dir:*
Albert D'Agostino, Alfred Herman. *Ed:*
William Swink. *Music:* Constantin Baka-
leinikoff. *With* Dennis O'Keefe (*Larry*),
Jane Greer (*Diane*), Lizabeth Scott
(*Joan*), Fay Baker (*Tilly*), James Bell
(*Mr. Neeley*), John Hoyt, Don Beddoe,
Marjorie Crossland, Bert Freed, Marjorie
Wood, Irene Tedrow, Virginia Farmer.
Prod: John Houseman for RKO. 83m.

THE RACKET (1951). One of Howard
Hughes' favourite projects about a tough

cop trying to eradicate civic corruption. *Sc:* William Wister Haines, W. R. Burnett (a story by Bartlett Cormack). *Ph:* George E. Diskant. *Art dir:* Albert D'Agostino, Jack Okey. *Ed:* Sherman Todd. *Music:* Mischa Bakaleinikoff. *With* Robert Mitchum (*Capt. McQuigg*), Lizabeth Scott (*Irene*), Robert Ryan (*Nick*), William Talman (*Johnson*), Ray Collins (*Welch*), Joyce MacKenzie (*Mary McQuigg*), Robert Hutton, Brett King ,William Conrad, Walter Sande, Les Tremayne, Don Porter, Walter Baldwin, Howland Chamberlain, Richard Karlan, Tito Vuolo, Isabel Jewell, Max Wagner. *Prod:* Edmund Grainger for RKO. 88m. Additional direction by Nicholas Ray. Re-make of *The Racket* (1929, Lewis Milestone).

THE GODDESS (1958). A savage, powerful, and effective tale of the rise and fall of a movie queen. *Sc:* Paddy Chayefsky (his story). *Ph:* Arthur J. Ornitz. *Art dir:* Edward Haworth. *Ed:* Carl Lesser. *Music:* Virgil Thompson. *With* Kim Stanley (*Emily Ann Faulkner*), Lloyd Bridges (*Dutch Seymour*), Steve Hill (*John Tower*), Betty Lou Holland (*The Mother*), Elizabeth Wilson (*The Secretary*), Bert Brinkerhoff, Gerald Hiker, Selene Walters, Joan Copeland, Bert Freed, David Whitney, Joyce Van Patten, Joan Granville, Donald McKee, Curt Conway, Patty Duke, Linda Soma, Kris Flanagan, Ray Sherman, John Lawrence, George Petrarca, Fred Herrick, Gail Haworth, Werner Klemperer, Margaret Brayton. *Prod:* Milton Perlman for Columbia. 105m.

THE SCAVENGERS (1959). An adventurer's stormy career and love life in Hong Kong. *Sc:* Edgar Romero. *Ph:* Felipe Sacdalan. *Ed:* Gervasio Santos. *Art dir:* Vincente Tomas. *With* Vince Edwards (*Stuart Allison*), Carol Omhart (*Maria Allison*), Tamar Benamy (*Marissa*), Efren Reyes (*Puan*), Vic Diaz (*O'Hara*), John Wallace (*Taggart*). *Prod:* Edgar Romero for Lynn-Romero. 79m. An American/Philippino co-production filmed in the Philippines.

DE SISTA STEGEN (U.S: A MATTER OF MORALS) (1960). A young American conformist tries unsuccessfully to adapt to life in Stockholm, ending up involved in robbery and murder. *Sc:* John D. Hess. *Phot:* Sven Nykvist (Agascope). *Ed:* Eric Nordern. *Art dir:* Bibi Lindström. *Music:* Dag Wiren. *With* Maj-Britt Nilsson (*Anita Anderson*), Patrick O'Neal (*Alan Kennebeck*), Mogens Wieth (*Erik Walderman*), Eva Dahlbeck (*Eva Walderman*), Gösta Cenderlund (*Eklund*), Claes Thelander, Lennart Lindberg, Hampe Faustman, Tord Peterson. *Prod:* John D. Hess, Steve Hopkins. *Prod:* Tom Younger for Fortress/United Artists. 90m.

Miscellaneous:

Although some sources list *Hidden Fear* (1956, Andre de Toth), and *If I Were Free* (1934, Elliott Nugent) as films on which Cromwell worked, he denies any participation in either. He did work for a week on *The Adventures of Marco Polo* (1938, Archie Mayo, John Ford), but was replaced.

A Thirties portrait of John Cromwell

MERVYN LE ROY: Star-making, Studio Systems and Style

"I believe in good scripts—I never start until I have the first and last page. And I always tried to help young players—Clark Gable would have been in *Little Caesar,* but the front office thought his ears were too big."
[Mervyn LeRoy talking to John Gillett at "Cinema City," London, 1970]

In recent years, the producer-director has come into his own, but in the latter days of the silent cinema, when Mervyn LeRoy was serving his apprenticeship as a director, the function of producer was non-existent, only becoming a recognised position once sound films had been established. At first, they were called supervisors, and were little more than front-office budget controllers, but men like David O. Selznick and Mervyn LeRoy envisaged a larger role and fought for a wider measure of control over their films.

LeRoy attained critical success in the early Thirties at Warners, and initiated his career in the capacity of producer-director at that studio in the mid-Thirties before moving on to Metro. Few men have changed stream as successfully: certain projects in the latter days at Warners suggested an expansion and change of his outlook on film-making and the dramatic scope of his material. His undoubted talent as a producer and star-maker, and his knack for recognising potential, made him an outstanding success, both critically and financially, and bought him numerous awards from many countries.

He was born in San Francisco on 15th October, 1900. His father lost his prosperous export/import business in the 1906 earthquake and fire, and died four years later leaving little chance of

"I believe in good scripts. I never start until I have
the first and last page"—Mervyn LeRoy

formal education for his son. So LeRoy worked as a newsboy, attracting the attention of a stage star, Theodore Roberts, who found him a part in "The Deep Purple" [later filmed by Raoul Walsh], and he also appeared as a bootblack in "Little Lord Fauntleroy." He did some extra work in a Broncho Billy Anderson film, made at the old Essanay Studio at Niles, California, but it was in vaudeville that he made his bid for fame.

He was billed as "The Singing Newsboy" when he joined Grauman's "Chinatown by Night" show; he was afforded this opportunity after winning a contest at the San Francisco World Fair in 1915, giving the best imitation of Charlie Chaplin, whom he had observed at first hand when Chaplin's unit had been filming nearby that of Anderson. Grauman hired him to repeat the act in a show at the San Francisco Exposition of Art, and later gave him the singing spot; moving on, LeRoy teamed with Clyde Cooper, another young show-business hopeful, in an act called "LeRoy & Cooper, Two Kids and a Piano," and later spent two years in musical comedy with Gus Edwards as part of "The Nine Country Kids" act. Finally, he ended up in Hollywood where he asked his cousin, Jesse Lasky, for a job behind a camera.

His first assignment was folding wardrobe costumes for *Secret Service* (1919); his enthusiasm, energy and push soon led to promotion as a film tinter. A subsequent request to become an assistant director was refused, but he was offered a chance as an assistant cameraman after spending hours perfecting a shot of moonlight on water for a William C. DeMille film. Soon tiring of this thankless role, he decided to return to vaudeville, but within a year he returned to Hollywood as a juvenile actor. He acted by day and attended night school in the evenings; he soon came to realise that acting was a hazardous profession, and turned his attention behind the cameras again. He befriended director Alfred E. Green who gave him an opportunity as a gag-man, and in this capacity he became a great friend of actress Colleen Moore; LeRoy has always held that these two people were responsible for launching his career.

Colleen Moore's husband, John McCormick, was then General Manager of First National Studios, and in 1927 plans were announced for LeRoy to direct Mrs. McCormick in a film entitled *Peg O' My Heart* or *Smiling Irish Eyes,* but the project fell through when McCormick fell from favour and resigned. But luck was on LeRoy's side, and he was assigned a comedy called *No Place to Go,* starring the popular Mary Astor, and its success led to a string of comedies and jazz-baby dramas featuring Alice White and Colleen Moore. Their content was slender, but successive contemporary reviews pointed out his growing skill in developing his material. The first wholly dramatic film he made was an early talkie, *Numbered Men* (1930), dealing with the effect of imprisonment on a variety of characters, which was praised for the atmosphere of exterior scenes filmed on a prison farm.

Gangsters as predominant figures or heroes have been traced back to D. W. Griffith's *The Musketeers of Pig Alley* (1913), but the vogue had not caught on until Josef von Sternberg's stylised accounts of their lives in *Underworld* (1927) and *The Docks of New York* (1928). LeRoy's *Broadway Babies* (1929) revolved around the temporary attractiveness of their sordid *milieu* for the heroine, but the film which made his name was something else. *Little Caesar* (1930) was drawn from the newspaper headlines; it blazed a trail with its reality, its violence and lack of concern for human life; but above all else, for the authenticity of its portrayal of the activities and hierarchy of organised crime. The ethnic and family-orientated customs and loyalties that it openly portrayed became iconographical features of the *genre,* along with the new status acquired by guns, cars and telephones; Edward G. Robinson rocketed to overnight fame at the forefront of a new

breed of actors who revitalised styles of film acting. His egoma-
niacal thug whose rapid climb to power resulted in an escalation
of violence and crime that swamped an entire city gave birth to
a whole host of imitators, of whom Paul Muni was probably one
of the best [in *Scarface* (1932)] and Lew Ayres one of the worst
[in *Doorway to Hell* (1930)], although Robinson retained the
lead, polishing and improving it at every outing.

The criminal's rise in social standing was reflected in the tux-
edos that replaced the heavy-shouldered uniform suits and in the
desire to assimilate culture by awkward visits to operas or theatres. Officials obsequiously paid lip service along the path of their
corruption; honest cops fumed in helpless rage while civic dig-
nitaries shouted for action but at the same time rubbed shoulders
with the new elite; and rich heiresses and playboys looked for
thrills in their company but soon found their patronising airs
changing to shudders as they got in too deep. In the end, it was
greed; power-mad lusting for *more* that put the skids under the
hoods, and sent them hurtling to their doom, shot down in the
gutters of the hard streets where they once ruled. W. R. Burnett's
Rico, the "Little Caesar," also displayed latent homosexual ten-
dencies, in keeping with the more flamboyant sexual aberrations
of *Scarface*: the outspoken nature of the film points to LeRoy's
persuasive abilities in that he was able to make the film unhin-
dered by the front office.

The individual efforts of Hal B. Wallis and Darryl F. Zanuck
as the leading Warner Brothers producers, and the style of directors like Curtiz and LeRoy were undoubtedly responsible for the
success of the company's fast-paced, machine-gun-dialogued and so-
cially-conscious output reaching the screen and attracting such vast
audiences. Not all of their creations were original, they copied
and assimilated as much as they were copied and assimilated;
Warner Brothers' prolific output included many re-makes [*20,000*

LeRoy rehearses Loretta Young and Grant Withers
in TOO YOUNG TO MARRY

Years in Sing Sing (1932) became *Castle on the Hudson* (G.B.:
Years and Days) (1940); *Taxi!* (1932) became *Waterfront* (1939)],
and some were so similar in their presentation that they
must have been made from the same shooting scripts, or following
constant viewings of the original!

Oddly enough, LeRoy's next film was made on loan to Metro:
Gentleman's Fate (1931) starred the ill-fated John Gilbert as a
snobbish socialite who turns to gangsterism. In spite of some rous-
ing action set-pieces, it was not a popular success, although British reviewers commented favourably on the recording of Gilbert's
voice. Back on the Warner lot, he was re-teamed with Francis
Faragoh, who wrote the screenplay for *Little Caesar,* and assigned
a film entitled *Too Young to Marry*. The original play, "Broken
Dishes," had served as a vehicle for Bette Davis's Broadway *début*

in 1929; the film version ironically (and very happily for the publicity department) starred Loretta Young and Grant Withers.

LeRoy had discovered Loretta Young in 1926; she and her sisters had been extras since 1917, but had stopped working while they attended convent school. According to an article by Ronald L. Bowers in "Films in Review" (April 1969):

"One day in 1926, Mervyn LeRoy telephoned the Young residence to ask if Polly Ann could report the next day for a child part in the Colleen Moore vehicle, *Naughty but Nice*. 13 year old Gretchen [later Loretta] answered the phone, and after telling LeRoy that Polly Ann was working on another picture, asked: 'Would I do?' LeRoy answered yes, and she played a bit in a group scene and received $80.00."

On January 26th 1930, Miss Young eloped by aeroplane to Yuma, Arizona, with Grant Withers, marrying him in the face of parental opposition. During the filming of *Too Young to Marry* in which they co-starred as a couple who marry in the face of parental opposition Miss Young had left Withers and was suing for divorce; the coincidental fusion of real life and film life was given widespread publicity by Warner Brothers.

LeRoy followed up with the first of a number of movies he made with rubber-mouthed, friendly comic Joe E. Brown, who was supported in *Broad-Minded* by a cast including Thelma Todd and Bela Lugosi. *Five Star Final* was the most substantial of LeRoy's projects, made during 1931: LeRoy was almost as prolific as Curtiz, turning out 36 films for Warners and First National in nine years.

Although it was based on the prototype of Lewis Milestone's *The Front Page* (1930), one can appreciate LeRoy's quoted remark about scripts in the context of this film. There are the usual racy wisecracks about sex and religion, but basically it is a serious work, condemning the use of sensationalism and muck-raking to sell papers, and as such it is played to the hilt by an experienced cast. The money-grubbing desires of the managing editors rub off on to the city editor, Randall (Edward G. Robinson), the familiarity with cheap methods arming him with equally cheap cynicism. He orders his reporters to stir up interest in a twenty-year-old case involving a young girl who killed her lover. She has since re-married, and gives one of the reporters—a defrocked clergyman, played with theatrical relish by Boris Karloff—a photograph of her daughter, Jenny (Marion Marsh), mistaking him for the clergyman officiating at Jenny's forthcoming wedding. LeRoy uses split screen photography to telling effect as the frantic mother pleads uselessly with Randall, after she has discovered her error. He has pangs of conscience when the parents commit suicide, and in a grim climax he is fired and returns to his office to find Jenny waiting to kill him, but he manages to convince her of his change of heart.

The topicality of Warners' material and its direct appeal to the working classes set it apart from the other studios. What their films lacked in comparison with the gloss of M-G-M or the sophistication of Paramount was more than adequately compensated for by their punch, and their presentation of everyday material which entertained the working classes because they could identify with the situations, the people and their surroundings, and the studio output was so prolific that everyone was catered for. Escapism was tempered with a measure of familiarity and reality. The public's virtues, vices and predilections became a common domain—the idle rich were mocked, crooked bankers and politicians met their downfall, secretaries won the hearts of their bachelor bosses, or immorally climbed to the heights until morality extracted its price, reporters and honest cops cleaned up gangsters, war heroes found the going tough, minorities fought against prejudice, and chorus girls danced and quipped their way to stardom seven nights a week. These dramatisations of the country's life reflected a social critique on a scale unprecedented or repeated since the Thirties by any other studio. The inherent truth of the tragic consequences of scandalmongering shown in *Five Star Final* gave LeRoy's film a depth and seriousness of purpose, whether or not this was intended or merely used as a dramatic device.

● ● ●

"We were highly organised and we wanted to keep working. There was a kind of creative excitement then; lots of good players like Robinson, Bogart, Cagney, Joan Blondell . . . and I always worked closely with the writers." [LeRoy talking to John Gillett at "Cinema City," London 1970]

LeRoy's *Two Seconds* (1932) and *Big City Blues* (released in June 1932, but probably made at the end of 1931) offer a total contrast, and accurately pinpoint the predicament of belonging to the Warner Brothers stable. Speed and economy were the key factors of their house style. *Two Seconds* is a major work; *Big City Blues* is a minor but very competent piece; both lack the overall conception and prominent social indictment of *I Am a Fugitive* (1932), but in their individual ways they serve specific purposes. *Two Seconds* offers Edward G. Robinson a *tour-de-force* role, while as a programmer *Big City Blues* is obviously aimed at a hick audience, to confirm the general view of big cities as corrupt dens of vice, but is sufficiently sustained to go down well with city dwellers. Neither Linden or Blondell carry the impact or range to make it work on the level of full-blooded, semi-tragic melodrama; nor do they have time, as it runs just over the hour.

The action takes place within a cycle of days with Indiana country boy Linden seen leaving his home town for New York, laughing at the scepticism of the booking office clerk, who had been there twenty-five years earlier and was glad that he had not stayed. On arrival, Linden falls prey to his cousin, a fast-talking

LeRoy rehearses a party scene for BIG CITY BLUES with
(left to right) Eric Linden, Inez Courtney, Humphrey
Bogart, Joan Blondell, Gloria Shea, Lyle Talbot, LeRoy
and unidentified figure

con merchant (Walter Catlett) with a habit of leaving his companion to pay the bills. A meeting with chorus girl Blondell leaves
Linden starry-eyed, and the romance is furthered during a wild
party in his hotel room.

LeRoy makes some sly cracks at Prohibition with the characterisation of the dimwitted hotel detective (Guy Kibbee), who
prowls the corridors between nipping into the laundry room for
a quick reviving shot. One of the guests at the party is confident-
ly played by a young Humphrey Bogart, displaying many of the
mannerisms of his later roles, especially a sardonic humour; he
is involved in a fracas which leaves a chorus girl lying dead in
Linden's room.

Linden goes on the run, meeting an ageing matron who takes him to a club where he re-establishes contact with Blondell, who had fled the party, but soon they are arrested and grilled as murder suspects; only the accidental discovery of the real killer's body in the laundry room [where he has hung himself] by Kibbee on a tippling trip, clears them and allows Linden to return to Indiana.

The camera placement and lighting by James Van Trees is mostly mundane, but suddenly in the parting sequence at the station there is a striking medium-close shot of Blondell, tearfully pressing herself against the bars of the ticket barrier . . . trapped in the prison of New York?

Robinson in *Two Seconds* is trapped in the four walls of a room in a dingy lodging house, which he shared with his pal (Preston Foster, whom LeRoy had signed for the role after seeing him in the stage version), a fellow scaffolder killed in a dramatic spiralling fall after a row with Robinson. Censorship being lax at the time, the dialogue made no bones about the profession of Blondell in *Big City Blues;* nor are any punches pulled in the characterisation of the gold-digging, sluttish, "dance hostess" (Vivienne Osborne) who tricks Robinson into marriage, contemptuously flinging him the odd dollar from her earnings when he is lying around the room: a broken man, riddled with guilt and self-loathing.

His performance starts on a muted key, depicting him as slow but hard-working and ambitious, then soon, in true style, he is contemptuously calling pedestrians beneath his scaffold "flies." He falls hard for the girl, and the farcical marriage scene with him paralytically drunk would have given the censor a headache a few years later. The death of Foster and the abstract low-key lighting with a single spot illuminating Robinson's face leaving the judge and jury barely discernible in the gloom at his trial, plus a strange shot of Osborne (photographed through a bed-frame) as she stands gloating over the prone figure of Robinson on the bed, squeezing her breasts against the head of the bed in joy, provide the visual high-points of the film, but in the closing segment visual style is surrendered in favour of close-ups of Robinson, mouthing insanely about the morality of his killing Osborne.

Once again, the film is structured in a circular fashion, beginning with reporters watching as Robinson is led in to the electric chair; a flashback begins with the surge of the current; and the film ends with a cut back to the reporters. The framework of a cycle of events also marked *I Am a Fugitive from a Chain Gang,* in which Paul Muni gave the first of several outstanding performances under LeRoy's direction; it is so well known that I do not propose to comment on it at length; it is notable for the single-minded, succinct quality with which it tenaciously makes its plea, for once cutting out the comic element that usually crept into Warner dramas and for the evergreen power of the ending as Muni answers his girl's query about how he lives, with a hissed: "I steal!" before vanishing into a pool of darkness.

Hard to Handle (1933) was a wildly paced Cagney vehicle, produced and co-scripted by another prolific figure behind the Warner Brothers cameras, Robert Lord. Cagney's skill in depicting decidedly unpleasant people with such verve, energy and humour that they became acceptable as normal heroes, was again exploited to the full. He appeared as a professional con-man whose contemptuous attitude to the public was summed up in his description: "The public is like a cow bellowing to be milked."

He is first seen running a dance marathon; the weary, jaded state of exhaustion displayed by the contestants and the heartless encouragement of the audience for their favourite couples catches the flavour of Horace McCoy's depressing "They Shoot Horses,

Don't They?," although it is played as much for comedy effect, heightened by LeRoy's insistence on detail and atmosphere. When a winner is found, but Cagney's partner has skipped with the prize money, the film starts to follow the regular pattern of a Cagney vehicle with the camera tracking away from a mob hot in pursuit of Cagney.

But then the difference emerges; it is not just one unlucky stunt that has gone wrong, but the fact that in spite of his bubbling confidence and quick tongue, and his seemingly inexhaustible energy, Cagney is being characterised as a loser. A scheme for a crooked treasure hunt at a fun fair [Cagney to promoter: "I'll sell you something that will swell your heart to the size of a peanut"] results in a riot; his efforts to sell non-rub face cream as reducing cream bring him to the attention of a bigger dealer, and his promiscuous daughter (Claire Dodd: "The Old Man's rather difficult to lay hands on, but I'm different that way!"). A grapefruit swindle lands him in the hands of the District Attorney until Cagney turns the tables by using grapefruit to promote a slimming campaign to glut the market and save his creditors.

LeRoy combines in-jokes such as Cagney to the D.A.: "I never even saw a grapefruit!" [Remember Mae Clarke earning his displeasure in *Public Enemy* (1931)?] with the hilarious comedy arising from Cagney's efforts to win the heroine from the domination of her fearsome, money-obsessed and socially-climbing mother, played by Ruth Donnelly ["I'd marry Tarzan of the Apes for a year's rent!"]. Pace, fluidity and an excellent script and cast tend to disguise LeRoy's visual sense, but the film is definitely one of his most underrated works of the Thirties.

Fluidity is not one of the key qualities of *Three on a Match* (1933), which uses the superstition about a third person taking a light to serve as a basis for an involving little drama, utilising three studio contract actresses. The quantitive demands of War-

ner output enabled the studio to exercise both subtle and un-
subtle pressures on their contract players, utilising their abilities
quite ruthlessly, relying on a suspension system by which time on
suspension was added to the length of the contract and the competitive nature of casting whereby, if an actress turned down or
resisted a part, there were plenty of others on hand to step in.
As an actress was only as good as her last picture, she had no
option but to work, the only advantage being, from her point of
view, that she could gain experience in a greater number of parts,
but even then there was a danger of type-casting.

The three ladies in *Three on a Match*, Joan Blondell, Bette
Davis and Ann Dvorak, are a case in point. Blondell specialised
in wise-cracking gold diggers with a big heart and bust to match;
Davis was a sharp-featured blonde, whose profile and style suggested push and determination; Dvorak was an excellent, dewy-
eyed "fallen woman." All three played some excellent parts, but
all frequently had to struggle to make something out of nothing.
In this film the latter applied to Davis's nanny role, but she and
Blondell were to stay the course at Warners while Dvorak, sadly,
did not.

The film opens with a montage of newspaper headlines to set
the film in its social and historical context; a scene with the trio
at school ends with a prediction that one will end up at reform
school, leading immediately into a shot of the grown girl, Joan
Blondell, *in* reform school. The unflagging pace is maintained as
rich Dvorak's marital unhappiness is betrayed by a shot of her
feigning sleep as her husband attempts to talk to her; the camera
follows his gaze to a mirror beside the bed, catching her with
her eyes perceptibly open. Soon she has fallen for Mike (Lyle
Talbot) a layabout wolf: her descent is graphically depicted by
a shot of her lying drunk and tousled on a bed, surrounded by
drink and cigarette butts. Blondell's efforts to help end with her

marrying Dvorak's ex-husband and engaging Davis as nanny.

The camera pans along with Dvorak's child from the marriage, playing in the park, cutting away to Davis and then to a muffled figure on a bench: once he is revealed as *Mike*, the cross-cutting increases suspense. Although the narrative development is patchy, the combination of camera movements and dialogue in neat transitions enforce intelligent points without any need for elaboration; the sets starkly create the pitiless *milieu* of grimy back streets and cheap hotels, populated by a sordid band of losers who struggle grimly but uselessly to change their luck. The disenchanted and the disinherited eke out their painful existence, hiding behind cynicism and cheap, unfulfilled promises. The climax is brilliantly handled: a drunken, frightened Dvorak comes to her senses

The moment of truth: Ann Dvorak and lipstick in
THREE ON A MATCH

after seeing her reflection in a mirror; hearing police sirens wailing in the street below as they search for her kidnapped child, she spectacularly commits suicide, crashing through a window to the street, with a message scrawled on her nightdress in lipstick pinpointing the kidnapper's position. Yet again the reality and exactness of the atmosphere lend themselves to a framework of social criticism without the latter necessarily being the motivating factor.

This social criticism was apparent in the classic *Gold Diggers of 1933,* although in a much more relaxed framework; the spectacular staging of the Busby Berkeley routines tends to divorce the plot and LeRoy's skilful direction from the mass of material written about the film. It contains an outstanding performance from Aline MacMahon as Trixie, the most hard-boiled of the heroines; to my mind, her exceptional quality as a performer has too long been neglected. Although LeRoy did not actually discover her, he built up her career over the years with small roles in *Five Star Final* (1931), *Heart of New York* (1932) and *The World Changes* (1933), the latter providing an especially telling role as the mother of Paul Muni, an immigrant who makes good in America, appearing briefly in the early stages, then fading out presumably having died, only to return at the climax—very convincingly made-up to represent extreme old age—to light up the screen with a blasting condemnation of the selfish and ungrateful behaviour of Muni's relations and children towards him.

She came into her own the following year with the lead in LeRoy's *Heat Lightning,* an arresting dramatic character study, played out in the heat of the Arizona desert. The detailed background strengthened the sentiments of the story, and MacMahon turned the psychology of her part into a dramatic performance of quiet strength and tender poignancy that held the film together with the subtlety of her acting. As a middle-aged woman with a

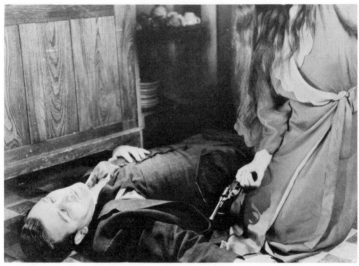

Aline MacMahon metes out rough justice to Preston Foster
in LeRoy's HEAT LIGHTNING

past, who tries to prevent her younger sister (Ann Dvorak) from
becoming involved with a petty crook (Preston Foster) with mur-
derous results, she was able to heighten and round out the in-
flections of her previous roles: secretaries holding back their un-
requited instincts selflessly, through a long-suffering loyalty, touching and sympathetic persons with a genuine warmth. Tay Garnett
in *One Way Passage* (1932), was able to draw these qualities in
her playing, but after LeRoy left Warners, MacMahon's career
drifted back into competent but wasted supporting roles.

LeRoy developed some of the same skills in his handling of

LEROY

Josephine Hutchinson in *Happiness Ahead* (1934), a musical co-starring her with Dick Powell, and *Oil for the Lamps of China* (1935). The latter was one of the turning points of his career at Warner Brothers in that it gave the first indication of his desire to landscape his material. Whereas the average Warner film ran seventy to eighty minutes, *Oil for the Lamps of China* ran 110; the timespan of the narrative was far more compressed than, say, *The World Changes,* but this was an adaptation of a popular novel, and the film script revealed several significant changes. Firstly, it suggested a more paternalistic 'Company' than that of the ruthless, impersonal organisation of the original; secondly, the novel criticised the futility of attempts to apply Western methods to Oriental modes of working and living, but the film suggested that the 'Company' had successfully made advances in enlightening the Chinese. Finally, a happy ending was tacked on; jilted Pat O'Brien had dedicated his life to the 'Company,' met and married Hutchinson as a semi-business partnership, rather than a relationship, suffered the death of his child and sundry indignities only to be demoted after saving the 'Company's' funds from marauding bandits, but in the film his value is finally realised.

LeRoy cleverly employs a montage sequence to suggest the ravages of the cholera epidemic that claims the life of O'Brien's child, but surprisingly suggests off-screen a fire sequence earlier in dramatic juxtaposition to the birth of the child. Performances are generally outstanding. O'Brien is excellent as an over-zealous man, dedicated to the belief that there are two things in a man's life: his wife and his job—and if the one fails him, he is lost with only the other. Josephine Hutchinson is frequently moving as the loyal wife who starts out believing it too but gradually stops loving him, and the supporting cast is strengthened by Arthur Byron as O'Brien's ideal boss, Donald Crisp as a tough Scot, and John

Eldredge as his weak right-hand man.

Tony Gaudio's first-rate high-key photography includes a number of foreground compositions such as the first meeting between O'Brien and Hutchinson, and establishes an atmosphere of a sticky unbearable climate with the use of white as a predominant colour (i.e. the Company employees' suits), and set-ups such as O'Brien's office where one is constantly aware of a roof-top fan, remorselessly revolving, even though it is often off focus or suggested by the use of shadow, while the spareness of Leo Forbstein's music direction is displayed by overlaying motifs from records into the background of subsequent scenes.

Movement in the film is geometrically precise: the camera pans between the wall partition of two offices as O'Brien hears Eldredge deal brusquely with an important Chinese customer; as the man leaves, O'Brien follows and intercepts him after which Eldredge enters from his office to complain in racial terms about being shown up, completing a triangular movement. Some time later, as the two men bid farewell to their wives on a staircase, the shot is composed so that O'Brien is above, dominating the figure of Eldredge.

Setting aside the thematic differences between novel and film, the latter is well staged and entertaining, although perhaps slightly too repetitive in making its main point. *Page Miss Glory* (1936) was not nearly as successful or entertaining, mainly due to Marion Davies's inability to cope with the timing of comedy dialogue; *I Found Stella Parish,* which followed, sounds like a promising weepie with a *tour de force* role for Kay Francis, and *Sweet Adeline* was also well thought of and had the added bonus of Irene Dunne singing. But all three were just marking time for LeRoy to embark on his most ambitious work of the Thirties, *Anthony Adverse* (1937).

Sheridan Gibney, from whose story *The World Changes* had

been adapted, spent five months writing the script from the massive novel on which it was based, and three months had been taken up with the casting. LeRoy insisted on the character of Anthony Adverse being changed from a passive one to a man of action so that his presence would hold together the many strands of the plot, as for once he felt he was offered a story that had *too many* possibilities. Critical response was divided over length and pacing with some feeling that the connections between the significant scenes were too slowly delineated, while others felt that the film lacked substance or point. It is a sprawling but *busy* picture, well directed and with some lively performances complementing its technical excellence.

Art director Anton Grot, quoted in the press book when it was released, had this to say of the film's 131 sets: "From my standpoint, the size of the sets was by no means a major problem . . . it meant much less to me than the constantly changing locales.

One day LeRoy would want us to have ready a French Nunnery and the next an Italian Monastery, or one day a street in Cuba and the next a street in Livorno, Italy. The detail that had to be watched was infinite."

The novel's adaptation left a third of the material untouched as there were plans for a sequel, but nothing ever came of them. The splendour of the varied settings tends to distract from rigid attention to the plot, but the film is always more than a set of tableaux thanks to the performances headed by a mature and full-blooded Fredric March, a gay and gracious Olivia de Havilland, a plaintive but appealing Anita Louise, a flamboyant Louis Hayward and an arch Claude Rains as the villain, while Gale Sondergaard won an Oscar for Best Supporting Actress as chief villainess, and another Oscar went to the editor, Ralph Dawson.

The opening sequences of LeRoy's next work, *They Won't*

Forget (1937), evoke the Civil War and the noble sentiments of Lincoln and Lee as a meaningful prelude to a stinging attack on prejudice and mob law. Lana Turner makes a big impact, jauntily swinging her tightly-sweatered bust to parade music in a star-making sequence; District Attorney Claude Rains waits impatiently for a big break to vote him into the Governor's seat, and he cold-bloodedly exploits the subsequent murder of Turner to whip up Southern prejudice with the aid of an unscrupulous press, building up a case of purely circumstantial evidence against her teacher that wins him national fame.

The film's visual power retains its impact for modern audiences—the murder scene with the camera tracking into a close-up of Turner as she hears footsteps in the deserted typing school building, cutting to a low angle shot of a man's feet at the door and his shadow, dissolving into a bugler playing the Last Post; overhead and angled compositions for the discovery of the body in the lift shaft, and the police interrogation of a terrified negro janitor; the dissolve from the blank space on the murder chart in Rains' office to teacher Edward Norris fixing his tie in a mirror, and the mailsack metaphor for the off-screen lynching. Le-Roy even filmed one shock cut in the courthouse scene without telling any of the cast bar Rains so that the impact would be one of natural surprise for the camera to record.

He also captures the feeling and atmosphere of a small town where the barber shop is the centre of gossip. With scenes like the riot at the railway station when a New York lawyer arrives to defend Norris, or that of the reporters callously photographing Norris's wife as she faints, then stooping to pick her up and revive her so that they can trick her into unwise confidences about her husband's feeling of being an outsider in the South, he captures a frightening possibility of reality.

Although the picture made a star of Turner, it did little

for the leads but it clinched a deal for LeRoy to join M-G-M as a producer. He began modestly with a Marx Brothers comedy, and star vehicles for Paulette Goddard and Robert Taylor before embarking on the classic adaptation of *The Wizard of Oz* (1939) which broke box-office records, won many awards and is still in commercial distribution. Its outstanding success made the next step in LeRoy's career at M-G-M inevitable.

LeRoy returned to direction with *Waterloo Bridge* (1940). Three film versions have been made of this story, with Bette Davis, Leslie Caron and Vivien Leigh playing the ballet dancer who loves a soldier during the First World War, only to fall on hard times due to a series of classic misunderstandings and class prejudices, finally coming to a tragic end on Waterloo Bridge.

Slick professionalism and capable playing support LeRoy's version with Leigh and Robert Taylor. At one stage, Leigh comments to Robert Taylor: "Oh, darling, it's unreal, isn't it?." He assents to her comment on Hollywood's traditional view of Scotland—an immaculately photographed exterior, visually perfect in its evocation of an early morning ride in a buggy, moving through the mist—gives way to the proverbial dense fog setting over the Bridge for Leigh's suicide. It *is* unreal, but reality has little to do with the *genre* of "women's pictures"; they seldom reflect any accurate detail of their characters' *milieu,* but they do strongly picture the attitudes of contemporary audiences and censors—particularly in terms of socially acceptable and unacceptable modes of behaviour. Snobbery was seen to be put down or misguided—Taylor's mother (Gladys Cooper) haughtily comes to meet Leigh in London, and thinks she is drunk when the girl arrives late and dishevelled for the meeting; the audience knows Leigh has just read Taylor's name in a casualty list, and that she cannot find the strength to tell Cooper—but moral lapses must be punished, thus Leigh's circumstantial fall into prostitution can only result in a tragic ending. The latter sequence is tastefully filmed, with restraint and a maximum of suggestion—an offscreen voice propositions her, she moves on and the traffic headlights flash faster and faster across her face; then comes a screech of brakes and she has gone under the wheels of an ambulance, leaving only a good luck charm for Taylor and her friend to find as they search desperately for her.

Similarly, the report of Taylor's death is bound to be wrong; one *knows* he will return as does the hero of *Seventh Heaven* (seemingly from the dead). Sentiment and emotion wring the last tear from audiences. Leigh stands at her window, musing: "I suppose that he's gone now" [Not knowing that his leave has been extended by 48 hours]. The camera tracks into a close-up of her face as she spots him standing outside in the rain, and she goes wild with excitement, rushing to the door half-clothed as her friend (Virginia Field) calls after her: "You'll look better in a dress." Later, when she is in Scotland to meet his family (who now understand her strange meeting with Cooper), she wins their love, and the sheer exuberance of her feeling for Taylor is romantically underlined both visually and verbally by the image of them dancing to the tune "Sweetheart", oblivious of all else, and their last kiss as he says goodnight to which she responds: "Goodbye, my darling. Every parting is a little eternity." Once again, the audience is a step ahead of the hero in realising the implication of her reply: that she is too ashamed to marry him in the circumstances.

The radiant, blooming Leigh cannot put a foot wrong, and is ably supported by a tart, single-minded Maria Ouspenskaya as her ballet mistress, and the earthy humour of Virginia Field. Only the reliable C. Aubrey Smith could deliver such a line as "That badge is never going to suffer at your hands" as he accepts his prospective daughter-in-law with such candour and conviction as

Vivien Leigh surrounded by the lavish Gibbons
decor for WATERLOO BRIDGE

not to bring an audience down in fits of laughter. The best soap-
operas stand the passage of time on the strength of their casting;
so much depends on the depth and conviction of the cast in terms
of winning modern audience response.

Escape was aimed primarily at contemporary audiences. Part of
the anti-German propaganda which characterised American films

of the Forties before Pearl Harbour, the plot had a solid romantic core and was rounded out with traditional show-business and horror (premature burial) exploitation angles. The bleak pessimism and low-key lighting of the opening scenes in a Bavarian concentration camp in 1936, soon give way to the fairy tale snowy village populated by quaint comic opera types; the efforts of naive American Robert Taylor to find his German-born actress mother take him through stunningly decorated Nazi offices to the mountain villa of an American born countess, Norma Shearer ("I've been very lucky living on my mountain top above all that [Nazi atrocity]."). Her connections with a charming sophisticated German general, Conrad Veidt, make Taylor suspicious of her, but the emotional reunion of mother and son convinces her that she has to help him escape, and she does so at the sacrifice of their love, giving them valuable time by turning on her General (playing on the fact of his weak heart), berating him until he collapses and dies in her arms as she softly repeats his words: "I did what I had to."

The cultural association of Shearer and Veidt is much more interestingly played than the sudden romance that springs up between her and Taylor (who is a rather unlikeable hero); Nazimova, making her talkie *début*, is extremely moving as an unworldly actress who has the courage to oppose the Nazis openly, and Dutch actor Philip Dorn scores as a sympathetic Nazi doctor; the script effectively presents the wall of silence that blocks Taylor's search, and creates an atmosphere of fear, backed by LeRoy's powerful visual style (e.g., the inn sequence where suspicious Nazi police play cat and mouse with Taylor, watching him from behind pillars and another table before questioning him, then silently placing themselves outside the door ["We wanted to be *sure* you see your friend."]).

Random Harvest (1942) was LeRoy's second picture with

Greer Garson; his uncanny knack for spotting potential and casting probably prompted the decision to counter the genteel, desexed image that Louis B. Mayer was busy cultivating for her. Following her success in *Goodbye Mr. Chips* (1939, Sam Wood), M-G-M had rushed her into several quickies, but it was not until 1941 with William Wyler's *Mrs. Miniver* and LeRoy's *Blossoms in the Dust* that her career really moved into top gear; her teaming with Walter Pidgeon resulted in an enormous fan mail and she topped box-office popularity polls throughout the Second World War.

Blossoms in the Dust romanticised the character of Edna Gladney, a woman who ran foster homes and fought for the rights of illegitimate children in Congress on the grounds that "their parents were illegitimate and so was society if it would not alter its inbuilt prejudices"; her taxing struggles enabled the writers to have the lady's spirits ebb and flow accordingly but there was less balance in *Random Harvest*. Both films began with a dramatic sequence to capture the audience's imagination (e.g., the suicide of illegitimate Marsha Hunt in *Blossoms,* and Colman's escape from the asylum in *Random Harvest*), before embarking on their tugging of the heart strings.

LeRoy had M-G-M's First Lady of Saintly Virtue don a kilt and tights to display her legs in a lively, traditional jig; she also displayed a certain amount of irresponsibility (e.g., meeting Colman, a perfect stranger, and finding he is unhappy, she says: "If you don't like the asylum, you shouldn't be there"). And she promptly elopes with him when he defends her from unwelcome attentions; however she retains some of her moral ethics by refusing to share a room until they are married, answering his proposal with: "Don't ask me, please. I might take you up on it. I'm that shameless." After the birth of a child, a car accident in Liverpool restores his lost memory, and he returns to his inher-

ited home, and courtship with young Susan Peters (Colman: "My dear, you look adorable"; Peters: "Well, adore me. I can bear it!").

LeRoy restores some balance by undercutting the intense sentimentality with scenes such as Colman's parental enthusiasm meeting a total disinterest from the registrar. The natural coincidences of soap-opera build up: the baby dies, Garson goes to work as Colman's secretary, and they eventually enter a business marriage when he recognises her after he regains his memory but they are unable to fulfil their love until a chance visit to the area where they had lived together before the accident . . . when they find their previous home, an old cottage is still clean and intact . . . old memories are revived and all live happily ever after.

The performances are capable, and their sincerity helps overcome the stickier patches in the script; the sheer lavishness of the *décor* and design, the loud romantic score, and the measured pace of the acting, camerawork and narrative development, illustrate the difference between Warner and M-G-M product. For instance, the opening shot is a long, *slow* track in to the gate of the asylum through which Colman escapes, building up an increasing tension, while a similar shot in Alfred E. Green's *Union Depot* (G.B.: *Gentleman for a Day*) (1932) moves much faster, swooping and craning up and across the vast set, establishing character and atmosphere economically.

But LeRoy had not lost his visual sense, merely subordinated it to the style of his material as can be seen from a later shot: a doctor is talking to a couple who could possibly be the parents of the amnesiac Colman; we see their outline through a frosted window, and hear their barely audible voices; filming the se-

Greer Garson's song and dance seemingly causes
a riot in LeRoy's RANDOM HARVEST

quence in this manner is both stylish and it also suggests the narrative outcome of the event by excluding the audience.

After directing Garson again as *Madame Curie* (1943), LeRoy turned his hand to war-time propaganda with *Thirty Seconds Over Tokyo* (1944) which told the story of Ted Lawson, who skippered one of the first planes to bomb Tokyo and lost a leg in the process. Spencer Tracy effectively plays the General who co-ordinated the operation, and Lawson is presented with slightly sombre, boyish charm by Van Johnson. An exceptionally long film, it tries to cover similar ground to Cromwell's *Since You Went Away* by concentrating on the characters of the men and their wives but Trumbo's script lacks the scope and organisation of Selznick's, relying on embarrassing flashbacks to key events in Johnson and Phyllis Thaxter's married life as Lawson is delirious, or in the amputation sequence. The emotionalism is probably quite valid, I'm sure that men in war did have these thoughts, but it is so over-played that it is difficult to take seriously; the action in the air is excitingly filmed but lacks any tension in the Tokyo raid as they meet with no opposition bar a little flak, and the last two reels are taken up with a tribute to the Chinese who help them to safety after a crash in bad weather. Again, the Japanese are said to be hot on their heels, but remain unseen; instead we have scenes of Chinese children at a mission hospital singing "America" that come over as awkward propaganda, leaving one with an overall impression of disappointment at the opportunities that have been missed.

Homecoming was far more effective as nurse Lana Turner converts a narrow-minded society doctor (Clark Gable) to understanding the reasons for American involvement in the War; their affair is moving, but so is the position of Gable's wife (Anne Baxter) who has to live with the knowledge of it back home, and the tragic ending satisfies both censorship needs and credibility.

Homecoming was followed by a combination of melodramas, tailored to fit the personalities of the stars involved, and re-makes of past successes such as the picture-postcard prettiness of LeRoy's version of *Little Women* where the emphasis was all on heart and colour at the expense of credible acting performances. The musical re-makes, such as *Lovely to Look At* and *Rose Marie,* reunited LeRoy with Busby Berkeley but there was less emphasis on the mechanics of the numbers than on the vocal abilities of the singing stars. LeRoy must take some of the blame for these mistakes, although they reflect the general gulf between the major companies and their audiences that characterised American films in the post-war period.

Million Dollar Mermaid (G.B.: *The One Piece Bathing Suit*) (1952) was better than most; fact and fiction were merged in the tradition of the Hollywood fantasy machine in this biography of Annette Kellerman: her father teaches his lonely, crippled child to swim, and to have an appreciation of music and ballet as he believes music (i.e. culture) can be the source of great happiness. He vetoes showman Victor Mature's desire to exploit her —having her swim in a publicity stunt to publicise a boxing kangaroo! She rises to fame with lengthy swimming feats in England and America, undertaken to help her father financially and to persuade a Broadway producer to back her 'name' in a water ballet. Being arrested for indecent exposure and winning her case brings the publicity needed to launch her water ballet, but she loses Mature who resents 'art'! Pa consoles her ("That's the price a woman has to pay for success—he'll come back when he has something to offer"), and dies at the height of her success. She goes to Hollywood, where she is crippled again in an accident, but all ends well as Mature reappears—as the discoverer of Rin-Tin-Tin . . . !

The programme of events is much the same as in other stage

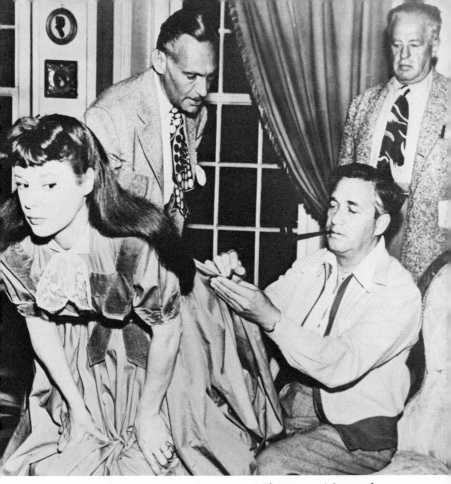

Mervyn LeRoy directs LITTLE WOMEN. Top (facing page) he stands, hand on bannister, rehearsing June Allyson below (cinematographer Robert Planck is behind her pointing finger). Left, he discusses *décor* designs with a member of the Art Department. Above, he pins up June Allyson's dress while discussing a production problem.

biographies, except that the 'numbers' are staged in water, under the guidance of Berkeley in one of his last flings with the gloriously spectacular Oyster ballet, dwarfing the routine plot. Folsey's mellow colouring, LeRoy's competent direction and capable performances, particularly by a less egocentric than normal Mature, help to make it a leisurely but entertaining film.

* * *

LeRoy's work in the latter half of the Fifties and Sixties has been largely confined to adaptations of stage successes, interspersed with the odd drama such as *The FBI Story* (1959); *The Devil at 4 O'Clock* (1961) and *Moment to Moment* (1966). Many of the former displayed an unhappy tendency toward excessive length or they padded out a basically funny situation beyond its endurance (e.g. *A Majority of One* [1961] or *Wake Me When It's Over* [1960]), tending to make one feel that LeRoy was better off in the Thirties when he had to work in the more restricted confines of the old Hollywood system when it was at its peak; in this competitive, highly-charged atmosphere he was better at spotting and making stars like Lana Turner, Jane Wyman, Loretta Young and Audrey Hepburn and the Dead End Kids, he was able to promote them in scripts that suited their personalities, whereas the paranoid Fifties signalled the death knell of the Old Hollywood, leaving directors like LeRoy to struggle with unsuitable material, assigned to them by virtue of their past reputations. The television directors who rose to fame like Lumet, Schaffner and Frankenheimer came from a background of limited schedules and demanding work quotas like those that LeRoy had experienced at Warners in the Thirties but it was unreasonable to suppose that the elder statesmen of Hollywood could break the habits of two decades and return to the frenetic style of their youth.

By the Seventies, these newcomers would also find the going

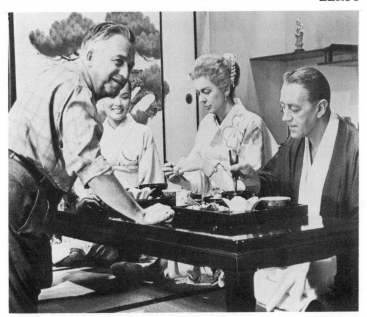

Mervyn LeRoy directs Rosalind Russell and
Alec Guinness in A MAJORITY OF ONE

tough as the film industry struggled through a series of set-backs
unimaginable in the heyday of the golden years of Hollywood,
with a major studio like M-G-M in virtual extinction. They have
survived, but with a far more uneven track record than Mervyn
LeRoy; some of their films sit unshown on the shelves in distrib-
utor's basements while *I Am a Fugitive from a Chain Gang, Gold
Diggers of 1933, They Won't Forget* and *The Wizard of* Oz are
aired time and time again in repertory cinemas and on television
for the enjoyment of new generations of film viewers.

MERVYN LE ROY Filmography

LeRoy appeared in one or more of Bronco Billy Anderson's films made at the Essanay studios at Niles, California, prior to 1915, as a child actor. No titles can be traced or remembered.

His first job in the movies was folding wardrobe for SECRET SERVICE (1919, Hugh Ford).

He acted on stage as a child, and from 1920 in the movies:

DOUBLE SPEED (1920, Sam Wood) as a juvenile.

?—a film with Betty Compson c.1920, title unremembered.

?—a film with Gloria Swanson c.1920, title unremembered.

THE GHOST BREAKER (1922, Alfred E. Green) as "A Ghost."

LITTLE JOHNNY JONES (1923, Arthur Rosson, Johnny Hines) as George Nelson.

GOING UP (1923, Lloyd Ingraham) as the Bellboy.

THE CALL OF THE CANYON (1923, Victor Fleming) as Jack Rawlins.

BROADWAY AFTER DARK (1924, Monta Bell) as Carl Fisher.

THE CHORUS LADY (1924, Ralph Ince) as 'Duke'.

From 1924, he moved behind the camera [he had spent six months as an assistant cameraman in 1921, after perfecting a shot of moonlight on water for William C. DeMille in an unremembered film] as a comedy writer, working on the comedy construction of following films: IN HOLLYWOOD WITH POTASH AND PERLMUTTER [GB: SO THIS IS HOLLYWOOD]. (1924, Alfred E. Green) as a gag writer.

SALLY (1925, Alfred E. Green).

THE DESERT FLOWER (1925, Irving Cummings).

THE PACE THAT THRILLS (1925, Webster Campbell).

WE MODERNS (1925, John Francis Dillon).

IRENE (1926, Alfred E. Green).

ELLA CINDERS (1926, Alfred E. Green).

"Boy, were we young!" is how LeRoy inscribed this shot of himself as an assistant director with star Ben Lyon as they study the script of THE PACE THAT THRILLS

IT MUST BE LOVE (1926, Alfred E. Green).

TWINKLETOES (1926, Charles Brabin).

ORCHIDS AND ERMINES (1927, Alfred Santell).

Miscellaneous:

In 1927, he was announced as the director of a film to be called PEG 'O MY HEART, but the project fell through. During his career, he worked on a number of films without taking credit, including the following:

THE DARK HORSE (1932, Alfred E. Green).

42ND STREET (1933, Lloyd Bacon), helping to film one of the numbers.

DESIRE ME (1947, no director credited). Filmed by George Cukor, but largely re-shot by Leroy.

THE GREAT SINNER (1949, Robert Siodmak), largely re-shooting and re-cutting the film.

THE GREEN BERETS (1968, John Wayne, Ray Kellogg), on which he spent five months helping John Wayne.

Director:

NO PLACE TO GO (1927). A banker's daughter takes her sweetheart bank clerk on a yachting trip to the South Seas to gratify her romantic desire to be wooed in an exotic setting. Memories of an experience with cannibals finally bring the couple together. *Sc:* Adelaide Heilbron (adapted from a "Saturday Evening Post" story, "Isles of Romance" by Richard Connell). *Ph:* George Folsey. *Titles:* Dwinelle Benthall, Rufus McCosh. *With* Mary Astor (*Sally Montgomery*), Lloyd Hughes (*Hayden Eaton*), Hallam Cooley (*Ambrose Munn*), Myrtle Stedman (*Mrs.*

Mary Astor and player in LeRoy's first film as a director, NO PLACE TO GO

Montgomery), Virginia Lee Corbin (*Virginia Dare*), Jed Prouty, Russ Powell. *Prod:* Henry Hobart for Henry Hobart Productions. Distributed by First National. 6,431 ft. 7r. This film is also known as *Her Primitive Mate*.

FLYING ROMEOS (1928). Barbers Cohen and Cohan take up flying to impress their manicurist girl friend; accidentally, they are hired to make an overseas flight, during the course of which their manicurist weds another pilot! *Sc:* John McDermott (his own story). *Ph:* Dev Jennings. *Ed:* Paul Weatherwax. *Titles:* Sidney Lazarus, Gene Towne, Jack Conway. *With* Charlie Murray (*Cohan*), George Sidney (*Cohen*), Fritzi Ridgeway (*Minnie*), Lester Bernard (*Goldberg*), Duke Martin (*The Aviator*), James Bradbury Jr., Belle Mitchell.

Prod: E. M. Asher for First National. 6,184 or 6,845 ft. 7r.

HAROLD TEEN (1928). Farm boy comes to city school, and turns the campus on its head by making a Western as an alternative to a school play, and accidentally blowing up a dam during filming! He also finds time to become a football hero. *Sc:* Thomas J. Geraghty (based on Carl Ed's comic strip, "Harold Teen"). *Ph:* Ernest Haller. *Ed:* LeRoy Stone. *With* Arthur Lake (*Harold Teen*), Mary Brian (*Lillums Lovewell*), Lucien Littlefield (*Dad Jenks*), Jack Duffy (*Grandpa Teen*), Alice White (*Giggles Dewberry*), Jack Eagan, Hedda Hopper, Ben Hall, William Bakewell, Lincoln Stedman, Fred Kelsey, Jane Keckley, Ed Brady, Virginia Sale. *Presented by:* Robert Kane. *Prod:* Allan Dwan for First National. 7,541 ft. 8r. Re-made in 1934 as *Harold Teen* [GB.: *The Dancing Fool*], directed by Murray Roth.

OH, KAY! (1928). Sailing on the eve of her wedding, the heroine falls into the hands of a rumrunner during a storm, but escapes and hides in a rich bachelor's mansion. She has to pose as his wife to evade a detective, and they decide to make the arrangement permanent (and legal). *Sc:* Carey Wilson (a play by Guy Bolton, Pelham Grenville Wodehouse, adapted by Elsie Janis). *Ph:* Sid Hickox. *Ed:* Paul Weatherwax. *Titles:* Pelham Grenville Wodehouse. *With* Colleen Moore (*Lady Kay Rutfield*), Lawrence Gray (*Jimmy Winter*), Alan Hale (*Jansen*), Ford Sterling (*Shorty McGee*), Claude Gillingwater (*Judge Appleton*), Julanne Johnston, Claude King, Edgar Norton, Percy Williams, Fred O'Beck. *Presented by:* John McCormick for First National. 6,100 ft. 6r.

NAUGHTY BABY (G.B.: RECKLESS ROSIE) (1929). A hat snatcher at a posh hotel sets her sights on a wealthy young bachelor, and sticks by him when his allowance is (temporarily) cut off, thus proving her love for him. *Sc:* Thomas Geraghty (a story by Charles Beahan, Garrett Fort). *Ph:* Ernest Haller. *Ed:* LeRoy Stone. *Titles:* Thomas Geraghty, Gerald Geraghty. *With* Alice White (*Rosalind McGill*), Jack Mulhall (*Terry Vandever*), Thelma Todd (*Bonnie Le Vonne*), Doris Dawson (*Polly*), James Ford (*Terry's pal*), Natalie Joyce, Frances Hamilton, Fred Kelsey, Rose Dione, Fanny Midgley, Larry Banthim, Georgie Stone, Benny Rubin, Andy Devine, Raymond Turner, Jay Eaton. *Presented by:* Richard A. Rowland for First National. 6,360 ft. 7r.

HOT STUFF (1929). Spinster Aunt sends a gas station pump girl to college, and encourages her to live it up; she only pretends to do so, and wins a sweetheart when her fraud is exposed. *Sc:* Louis Stevens (a story by Robert S. Carr). *Ph:* Sid Hickox. *Special Ph:* Alvin Knechter. *Art dir:* John Hughes. *Ed:* Terry Morse, Mervyn LeRoy(?). *Titles and add. dial:* Humphrey Pearson. *Costumes:* Max Ree. *With* Alice White (*Barbara Allen*), Louise Fazenda (*Aunt Kate*), William Bakewell (*Mack Moran*), Doris Dawson (*Thelma*), Ben Hall (*Sandy McNab*), Charles Sellon, Buddy Messinger, Andy Devine, Larry Banthim. *Presented by:* Richard A. Rowland. *Prod:* Wid Gunning for First National. 6,774 ft. (part sound); 7,466 ft. (silent). 7r.

BROADWAY BABIES (G.B.: BROADWAY DADDIES) (1929). The love life of a chorus girl involves a stage manager, a Canadian and a gambler in a dramatic series of events, resolved by a gang war; the result enables the chorus girl and her stage manager to finance their own Broadway show. *Sc:* Monte Katterjohn (a "Good Housekeeping" story, "Broadway Musketeers" by Jay Gelzer). *Dial:* Monte Katterjohn, Humphrey Pearson. *Ph:* Sol Polito. *Art dir:* Jack Okey. *Ed:* Frank Ware. *Titles:* Paul Perez. *Costumes:* Max Ree. *Song:* "Broadway Baby" ["Broadway Baby Doll"?] by Al Bryan, George W. Muzer. *With* Alice White (*Delight Foster*), Charles Delaney (*Billy Buvanny*), Fred Kohler (*Percé Gessant*), Tom Dugan (*Scotty*), Bodil Rosing (*Sarah Durgen*), Sally Eilers, Marion Byron, Jocelyn Lee, Louis Natheaux, Maurice Black. *Presented by:* Richard A. Rowland. *Prod:* Robert North for First National. 8,067 ft. (sound); 6,690 ft. (silent). 9r.

LITTLE JOHNNY JONES (1929). Fame and the bright lights of New York turn the head of a small town jockey, but he regains his sweetheart's love by going to England, and riding an Epsom winner. *Sc:* Adelaide Heilbron, Edward Buzzell (a play by George M. Cohan). *Dial:* Adelaide Heilbron. *Ph:* Faxon Dean. *Ed:* Frank Ware. *Songs:* "Yankee Doodle Dandy"; "Give My Regards to Broadway," by George M. Cohan; "Straight Place and Show" by Herman Ruby, M. K. Jerome; "Go Find Somebody to Love" by Herb Magidson, Michael Cleary; "My Paradise" by Herb Magidson, James Cavanaugh; "Painting the Clouds with Sunshine" by Al Dubin, Joe Burke. *With* Edward Buzzell (*Little Johnny Jones*), Alice Day (*Mary Baker*), Edna Murphy

(*Vivian Dale*), Robert Edeson (*Ed Baker*), Wheeler Oakman (*Wyman*), Raymond Turner, Donald Reed. *Prod:* First National. 6,621 ft. (sound); 5,020 ft. (silent). 8r. Re-make of 1923 film, directed by Arthur Rosson and Johnny Hines, in which LeRoy acted.

PLAYING AROUND (1930). Sheba Miller, a stenographer with a desire for luxuries, jilts her beau Jack in favour of a gangster; when they run out of money on their honeymoon, the gangster robs her father's cigar counter, wounding him, but Jack's identification leads to the gangster's arrest and a happy ending. *Sc:* Adele Commandini, Frances Nordstrom from (a story, "Sheba" by Viña Delmar). *Dial. and titles:* Humphrey Pearson. *Ph:* Sol Polito. *Songs:* "You're My Captain Kidd"; "That's the Lowdown on the Lowdown"; "We Learn About Love Every Day"; "Playing Around" by Sam H. Stept, Bud Green. *With* Alice White (*Sheba Miller*), Chester Morris (*Nicky Solomon*), William Bakewell (*Jack*), Richard Carlyle (*Pa Miller*), Marion Byron (*Maude*), Maurice Black, Lionel Belmore, Shep Camp, Ann Brody, Nellie V. Nichols. *Prod:* Robert Lord for First National. 66m.

SHOWGIRL IN HOLLYWOOD (G.B.: THE SHOWGIRL IN HOLLYWOOD). (1930). After a Broadway flop, the star is spotted and taken to Hollywood where she lands a leading role, but her displays of temperament nearly cause the picture to be cancelled, and this drives her girl friend to an unsuccessful suicide attempt which calms the star down, and the picture is finished successfully. *Sc:* Harvey Thew, James A. Starr (a novel, "Hollywood Girl" by Joseph Patrick

McEvoy). *Dial:* Harvey Thew. *Ph:* Sol Polito. *Art dir:* Jack Okey. *Ed:* Peter Fritch. *Songs:* "Hang on to the Rainbow"; "I've Got My Eye on You"; "There's a Tear for Every Smile in Hollywood" by Bud Green, Sammy Stept. *Music dir:* Leo Forbstein. *Dance dir:* Jack Haskell. *With* Alice White (*Dixie Dugan*), Jack Mulhall (*Jimmy Doyle*), Blanche Sweet (*Donna Harris*), Ford Sterling (*Sam Otis*), John Miljan (*Frank Buelow*), Virginia Sale, Lee Shumway, Herman Bing, Spec O'Donnell. *Prod:* Robert H. North for First National. 80m.

NUMBERED MEN (1930). Bud, a con serving ten years for counterfeiting, hears that another criminal, Rinaldo, is bothering his girl. She prevents Bud from making a break while serving on a prison farm, but he is suspected when Rinaldo is shot. The testimony of his pal clears Bud and reunites the lovers. *Sc:* Al Cohn, Henry McCarthy (a play, "Jailbreak" by Dwight Taylor). *Ph:* Sol Polito. *Art dir:* Jack Okey. *Ed:* Terrill Morse. *With* Conrad Nagel (*Bertie Gray*), Bernice Claire (*Mary Dane*), Raymond Hackett (*Bud Leonard*), Ralph Ince (*King Callahan*), Tully Marshall (*Lemuel Barnes*), Maurice Black, William Holden, George Cooper, Blanche Frederici, Ivan Linow, Frederick Howard. *Prod:* First National. 6,480 ft. 8r.

TOP SPEED (1930). A comedy about two vacationing bond clerks who become enmeshed in a crooked boat race, and are accused of a bond theft, but manage to clear themselves. *Sc:* Humphrey Pearson, Henry McCarty [*sic*] (a play by Bert Kalmar, Harry Ruby, Guy Bolton). *Ph:* Sid Hickox. *Ed:* Harold Young. *Songs:* "Goodness Gracious"; "I'll

Know and She'll Know"; "Keep Your Undershirt On"; "What Would I Care?"; "Sweeter Than You" by Bert Kalmar, Harry Ruby; "As Long As I Have You and You Have Me" by Al Dubin, Joe Burke. *With* Joe E. Brown (*Elmer Peters*), Bernice Claire (*Virginia Rollins*), Jack Whiting (*Jerry Brooks*), Frank McHugh (*Tad Jordan*), Laura Lee (*Babs Green*), Rita Flynn, Edwin Maxwell, Wade Boteler, Edmund Breese, Cyril Ring, Billy Bletcher, Al Hill. *Prod:* First National. 80m.

LITTLE CAESAR (1930). Classic story of the rise and fall of Rico Bandello from the ranks of the gangster establishment. *Sc:* Francis Faragoh (a novel by W. R. Burnett). *Ph:* Tony Gaudio. *Art dir:* Anton Grot. *Ed:* Ray Curtiss. *Music dir:* Leo Forbstein. *With* Edward G. Robinson ("*Rico*" *Bandello*), Sidney Blackmer (*Big Boss*), Glenda Farrell (*Olga Strassof*), Ralph Ince (*Pete Montana*), Douglas Fairbanks Jr. (*Joe Massara*), William Collier Jr., Thomas Jackson, Maurice Black, Sam Vettori, George E. Stone. *Supervised by:* Darryl F. Zanuck. *Prod:* Hal B. Wallis for First National. 80m.

GENTLEMAN'S FATE (1931). Young socialite finds his family are involved in the rackets, and follows their lead with tragic consequences. *Sc:* Leonard Praskins (a story by Ursula Parrott). *Ph:* Merritt B. Gerstad. *Art dir:* Cedric Gibbons. *Ed:* William S. Gray. *With* John Gilbert (*Jack Thomas*), Louis Wolheim (*Frank*), Leila Hyams (*Marjorie*), Anita Page (*Ruth*), Marie Prevost (*Mabel*), John Miljan, George Cooper, Ferike Boros, Ralph Ince, Frank Reicher, Paul Porcasi, Tenen Holtz. *Prod:* M-G-M. 90m.

TOO YOUNG TO MARRY (1931). Film version of stage success about a young couple who elope in the face of parental disapproval of their relationship. *Sc:* Francis Faragoh (a play, "Broken Dishes" by Martin Flavin). *Ph:* Sid Hickox. *Ed:* John Rollins. *Music dir:* Leo Forbstein. *With* Loretta Young (*Elaine Bumpstead*), Grant Withers (*Bill Clark*), O. P. Heggie (*Cyrus Bumpstead*), Emma Dunn (*Mrs. Bumpstead*), J. Farrell MacDonald (*The Reverend Mr. Stump*), Lloyd Neal, Richard Tucker, Virginia Sale, Aileen Carlisle. *Prod:* Warner Brothers. 67m. Some sources refer to this film as *Broken Dishes*.

BROAD-MINDED (1931). A college farce, featuring the popular comic Joe E. Brown. *Sc:* Bert Kalmar, Harry Ruby (their own story). *Ph:* Sid Hickox. *Ed:* Al Hall. *Music dir:* Leo Forbstein. *With* Joe E. Brown (*Ossie Simpson*), Ona Munson (*Constance Palmer*), William Collier Jr. (*Jack Hackett*), Marjorie White (*Penelope Packer*), Margaret Livingstone (*Mabel Robinson*), Thelma Todd, Bela Lugosi, Grace Hampton, Holmes Herbert, George Grandee. *Prod:* First National. 72m.

FIVE STAR FINAL (1931). Expose of muck-racking journalism and its often tragic results. *Sc:* Robert Lord (a play by Louis Weitzenkorn). *Add. dial:* Byron Morgan. *Ph:* Sol Polito. *Art dir:* Jack Okey. *Ed:* Frank Ware. *Music dir:* Leo Forbstein. *With* Edward G. Robinson (*Randall*), H. B. Warner (*Michael Townsend*), Marion Marsh (*Jenny Townsend*), Anthony Bushell (*Phillip Weeks*), Frances Starr (*Nancy Townsend*), George E. Stone, Ona Munson, Boris Karloff, Robert Elliott, Aline Mac-

Mahon, Purnell Pratt, David Torrence, Oscar Apfel, Gladys Lloyd, Evelyn Hall, Harold Waldridge, Polly Walters, James Donlin, Frank Darien. *Prod:* Hal B. Wallis for First National. 87m. Re-made as *Two Against the World* (1936, William McGann); alternative title for U.S. television showings is *One Fatal Hour*.

LOCAL BOY MAKES GOOD (1931). Joe E. Brown again as a shy botanist who has to become an athletic champ to win his secret love. *Sc:* Robert Lord (play "The Poor Nut" by J. C. Nugent, Elliott Nugent). *Ph:* Sol Polito. *Ed:* Jack Killifer. *Music dir:* Leo Forbstein. *With* Joe E. Brown (*John Miller*), Dorothy Lee (*Julia Winters*), Ruth Hall (*Marjorie Blake*), Edward Woods (*Spike Hoyt*), Edward J. Nugent (*Wally Pierce*), Wade Boteler, William Burress, John Harrington, Robert Bennett. *Prod:* Robert Lord for First National. 67m.

TONIGHT OR NEVER (1931). Gloria Swanson appeared as a prima donna, engaged to royalty but fascinated by a young stranger who comes into her life. *Sc:* Ernest Vajda (a play by Lili Hatvany). *Ph:* Gregg Toland. *Art dir:* Willy Pogany. *Ed:* Grant Whitlock. *With* Gloria Swanson (*Nella Vago*), Ferdinand Gottschalk (*Rudig*), Melvyn Douglas (*The Unknown Gentleman*), Robert Grieg (*Butler*), Greta Mayer (*Maid*), Warburton Gamble, Alison Skipworth, Boris Karloff. *Prod:* United Artists. 80 mins.

HIGH PRESSURE (1932). Fast-paced comedy with William Powell as a get-rich-quick type whose Golden Gate Artificial Rubber Company goes haywire when he discovers the idea has come from an unhinged inventor! *Sc:* Joseph

Jackson (a story by S. J. Peters). *Ph:* Robert Kurrle. *Ed:* Ralph Dawson. *Music dir:* Leo Forbstein. *With* William Powell (*Gar Evans*), George Sidney (*Colonel Ginsburg*), Evelyn Brent (*Francine*), Frank McHugh (*Mike Donoghey*), Guy Kibbee (*Clifford Gray*), Evalyn Knapp, Ben Alexander, Harry Beresford, John Wray, Charles Judels, Luis Alberni, Lucien Littlefield, Charles Middleton, Alison Skipworth, Lilian Bond, Maurice Black, Bobby Watson, Oscar Apfel, Polly Walters. *Prod:* Warner Brothers. 74m. Working title was *Hot Money*.

HEART OF NEW YORK (1932). A Jewish comedy about match-making, plumbing and inventing. *Sc:* Arthur Caesar, Houston Branch (play "Mendel, Inc." by David Freedman). *Ph:* James Van Trees. *Ed:* Terry Morse. *Music dir:* Leo Forbstein. *With* Joe Smith (*Sam Shtrudel*), Charles Dale (*Bernard Schnaps*), George Sidney (*Mendel Marantz*), Anna Appel (*Mrs. Mendel*), Ruth Hall (*Lillian Mendel*), Aline MacMahon, Ann Brody, Harold Waldridge, Marion Byron, Donald Cook, George MacFarlane, Charles Coleman. *Prod:* Warner Brothers. 78 m. Working title was *Mendel, Inc.*

TWO SECONDS (1932). The title refers to the space of time it takes for a man to die in the electric chair; convicted murderer Edward G. Robinson relives his life in flashback as the motives for his crime are revealed. *Sc:* Harvey Thew (a story by Lester Elliott). *Ph:* Sol Polito. *Art dir:* Anton Grot. *Ed:* Terrill Morse. *Music dir:* Leo Forbstein. *With* Edward G. Robinson (*John Allen*), Preston Foster (*Bud*), Vivienne Osborne (*Shirley*), J. Carroll Naish (*Tony*), Guy Kibbee

(*Bookie*), Adrienne Dare, Walter Walker, Dorothea Wolbert, Edward McWade, Berton Churchill, Lew Brice, Franklin Parker, Frederick Howard, Helen Phillips, June Gittelson, Jill Dennett, Luana Walters, Otto Hoffman, William Janney, Harry Beresford, John Kelly, Matt McHugh, Harry Woods, Gladys Lloyd. *Prod:* First National. 68m.

BIG CITY BLUES (1932). An excited country boy, visiting New York for the first time, falls into bad company, and is accused of murder. *Sc:* Ward Morehouse, Lillie Hayward (a story, "New York Town" by Ward Morehouse). *Ph:* James Van Trees. *Art dir:* Anton Grot. *Ed:* Ray Curtiss. *Music dir:* Leo Forbstein. *With* Joan Blondell (*Vida*), Eric Linden (*Bud*), Inez Courtney (*Faun*), Evelyn Knapp (*Jo-Jo*), Guy Kibbee (*Hummel*), Lyle Talbot, Gloria Shea, Walter Catlett, Jobyna Howland, Humphrey Bogart, Herman Bing, J. Carroll Naish, Tom Dugan, Grant Mitchell, Ned Sparks, Josephine Dunn, Thomas Jackson, Sheila Terry, Betty Gillette, Edward McWade, Gordon Elliott. *Prod:* Warner Brothers. 65m.

THREE ON A MATCH (1932). A fast-paced melodrama, outlining the changes in fortune of three school chums after they meet for a reunion. *Sc:* Lucien Hubbard (a story by Kubec Glasmon, John Bright). *Add. dial:* Kubec Glasmon, John Bright. *Ph:* Sol Polito. *Art dir:* Robert Haas. *Ed:* Ray Curtiss. *Music dir:* Leo Forbstein. *With* Joan Blondell (*Mary*), Warren William (*Henry*), Ann Dvorak (*Vivian*), Bette Davis (*Ruth*), Lyle Talbot (*Mike*), Grant Mitchell, Buster Phelps, Sheila Terry, Glenda Farrell, Clara Blandick, Humphrey Bogart, John

Marston, Patricia Ellis, Hale Hamilton, Herman Bing, Dawn O'Day (later Anne Shirley), Edward Arnold, Jack LaRue, Allen Jenkins, Frankie Darro, Virginia Davis, Dick Brandon. *Assoc. prod:* Sam Bischoff for First National. 64m. Re-made as *Broadway Musketeers* (1938, John Farrow).

I AM A FUGITIVE FROM A CHAIN GANG (GB: I AM A FUGITIVE FROM THE CHAIN GANG) (1932). Vivid so-

Paul Muni and Mervyn LeRoy relax between takes on I AM A FUGITIVE FROM A CHAIN GANG

cial document with Muni ideally cast as the First World War veteran who pays the penalty in a particularly savage and unjust manner when he tries to expose the inhumanity of his experiences while serving on a chain gang. *Sc:* Howard J. Green, Brown Holmes (a novel by Robert E. Burns). *Ph:* Sol Polito. *Art dir:* Jack Okey. *Ed:* William Holmes. *Music dir:* Leo Forbstein. *With* Paul Muni (*James Allen*), Glenda Farrell (*Marie*), Helen Vinson (*Helen*), Preston Foster (*Pete*), David Landau (*The Warden*), Edward J. McNamara, Sheila Terry, Allen Jenkins, Berton Churchill, Edward Ellis, Sally Blane, James Bell, John Wray, Hale Hamilton, Douglas Dumbrille, Roscoe Karns, Robert Warwick, Noel Francis, Charles Middleton, Irving Bacon, Russell Simpson, Oscar Apfel, Louise Carter, John Marston, Spencer Charters, Harry Holman, William Janney, Jack LaRue, Morgan Wallace, C. Henry Gordon, Reginald Barlow, Charles Sellon, George Collins, William Pawley, Lew Kelly, Edward Arnold, Sam Baker, William Le Maire. *Prod:* Hal B. Wallis for Warner Brothers. 93m.

HARD TO HANDLE (1933). Con-man Cagney, who believes 'the public is like a cow bellowing to be milked,' meets his match in hard-as-nails Ruth Donnelly as the mother of his sweetheart. *Sc:* Wilson Mizner, Robert Lord (a story by Houston Branch). *Ph:* Barney McGill. *Art dir:* Robert Haas. *Ed:* William Holmes. *Music dir:* Leo Forbstein. *With* James Cagney (*Lefty Merrill*), Mary Brian (*Ruth Waters*), Ruth Donnelly (*Lil Waters*), Claire Dodd (*Marlene Reeves*), Gavin Gordon (*John Hayden*), Allen Jenkins, Emma Dunn, Robert McWade, John

Sheehan, Matt McHugh, Louise Mackintosh, William H. Strauss, Bess Flowers, Lew Kelly, Berton Churchill, Harry Holman, Grace Hayle, George Pat Collins, Douglas Dumbrille, Sterling Holloway, Charles Wilson, Jack Crawford, Stanley Smith, Walter Walker, Mary Doran. *Prod:* Robert Lord for Warner Brothers/Vitaphone. 75m.

TUGBOAT ANNIE (1933). Rich characterisations by Dressler and Beery lift this comedy-drama above the cheap romanticism of the original story as they try to eke a living from their tugboat. *Sc:* Zelda Sears, Eve Greene (a story by Norman Reilly Raine). *Ph:* Gregg Toland. *Art dir:* Cedric Gibbons. *Ed:* Blanche Sewell. *With* Marie Dressler (*Annie*), Wallace Beery (*Terry*), Robert Young (*Alec*), Maureen O'Sullivan (*Pat*), William Robertson (*Severn*), Tammany Young, Jack Pennick, Paul Hurst, Frankie Darro. *Prod:* M-G-M. 87m.

ELMER THE GREAT (1933). One of several Joe E. Brown vehicles that featured the comedian as an expert baseball player; here he is a mulish braggart whose naivety leads him into bad company. *Sc:* Tom Geraghty (a play by Ring Lardner, George M. Cohan). *Ph:* Arthur Todd. *Ed:* Thomas Pratt. *Music dir:* Leo Forbstein. *With* Joe E. Brown (*Elmer Kane*), Patricia Ellis (*Nellie Poole*), Claire Dodd (*Evelyn Corey*), Preston Foster (*Dave Walker*), Frank McHugh (*High Hips Healy*), Sterling Holloway, Jessie Ralph, Russell Hopton, Emma Dunn, Charles Wilson, Berton Churchill, J. Carroll Naish, Lloyd Neal, Douglas Dumbrille, Gene Morgan, Charles Delaney. *Prod:* First National. 74m. Remake of *Fast Company* (1929, Edward Sutherland).

GOLD DIGGERS OF 1933 (1933). Social content and concentration on the comical pranks of the gold digging girls off-stage offer a lively variation of the traditional back stage musical *genre* in this classic entertainment. *Sc:* Erwin Gelsey, James Seymour (play, "Gold Diggers" by Avery Hopwood). *Add. dial:* David Boehm, Ben Markson. *Ph:* Sol Polito. *Art dir:* Anton Grot. *Ed:* George Amy. *Music and lyrics:* Harry Warren, Al Dubin. *Dance dir:* Busby Berkeley. *Songs:* "We're in the Money"; "Pettin' in the Park"; "My Forgotten Man"; "Shadow Waltz"; "I Want to Sing a Torch Song." *With* Warren William (*J. Lawrence*), Joan Blondell (*Carol*), Aline MacMahon (*Trixie*), Ruby Keeler (*Polly*), Dick Powell (*Brad*), Guy Kibbee, Ned Sparks, Ginger Rogers, Clarence Nordstrom, Robert Agnew, Tammany Young, Sterling Holloway, Ferdinand Gottschalk, Lynn Browning, Charles Wilson, Billy Party, Snowflake [Fred Toomes], Theresa Harris, Joan Barclay, Wallace MacDonald, Wilbur Mack, Grace Hayle, Charles Lane, Hobart Cavanaugh, Gordon Elliott, Dennis O'Keefe, Busby Berkeley, Fred Kelsey, Frank Mills, Ann Hovey, Barbara Rogers, Pat Wing, Loretta Andrews. *Prod:* Hal B. Wallis for Warner Brothers. 96m.

THE WORLD CHANGES (1933). Saga of a farm boy's rise to success as a wealthy businessman at the cost of personal happiness. *Sc:* Edward Chodorov (a story by Sheridan Gibney). *Ph:* Tony Gaudio. *Ed:* William Holmes. *Music dir:* Leo Forbstein. *With* Paul Muni (*Orin Nordholm Jr.*), Mary Astor (*Virginia Nordholm*), Aline MacMahon

(*Anna Nordholm*), Donald Cook (*Richard Nordholm*), Alan Dinehart (*Ogden Jarrett*), Guy Kibbee, Margaret Lindsay, Henry O'Neill, Jean Muir, Anna Q. Nilsson, Patricia Ellis, Willard Robertson, Douglas Dumbrille, Mickey Rooney, Clay Clement, Wallis Clark, Oscar Apfel, Sidney Toler, Alan Mowbray, Gordon Westcott, Arthur Hohl, William Janney, Philip Faversham, Jackie Searle, Marjorie Gateson, William Burress. *Prod:* Hal B. Wallis for Warner Brothers. 90m.

HEAT LIGHTNING (1934). A high-powered melodrama featuring Aline MacMahon and Ann Dvorak as two sisters in a small town whose involvement with two crooks leads to murder. *Sc:* Brown Holmes, Warren Duff (a play by George Abbott, Leon Abrams). *Ph:* Sid Hickox. *Art. dir:* Jack Okey. *Ed:* Howard Bretherton. *Music dir:* Leo Forbstein. *With* Aline MacMahon (*Olga*), Ann Dvorak (*Myra*), Preston Foster (*George Schaffer*), Lyle Talbot (*Jeff*), Glenda Farrell (*Mrs. Tifton*), Ruth Donnelly, Frank McHugh, Edgar Kennedy, Theodore Newton, Willard Robertson, Jane Darwell, Muriel Evans, Harry C. Bradley, James Durkin. *Assoc. prod:* Sam Bischoff for Warner Brothers. 63m. Re-made as *Highway West* (1941, William McGann).

HI, NELLIE! (1934). "Heart-throb" editor of a metropolitan daily ends up involved with gangsters, after the more banal aspects of his job have driven him to drink. *Sc:* Abem Finkel, Sidney Sutherland (a story by Roy Chanslor). *Ph:* Sol Polito. *Art dir:* Robert Haas. *Ed:* William Holmes. *Music dir:* Leo Forbstein. *With* Paul Muni (*Samuel N. Bradshaw*), Glenda Farrell (*Gerry Krale*), Ned Sparks (*Shammy*), Robert Barrat

(*Brownell*), Douglas Dumbrille (*Harvey Dawes*), Kathryn Sergava, Hobart Cavanaugh, Berton Churchill, Edward Ellis, Paul Kaye, Donald Meek, Dorothy Le Baire, Marjorie Gateson, George Meeker, Harold Huber, Allen Vincent, Pat Wing, Frank Reicher, George Chandler, George Humbert, Sidney Miller, James Donlan. *Prod:* Robert Presnell for Warner Brothers. 75m.

HAPPINESS AHEAD (1934). A musical comedy about a bored heiress who meets and falls in love with a window cleaner, and her subsequent efforts to pass herself off as a poor working girl. *Sc:* Harry Sauber, Brian Marlow (a story by Harry Sauber). *Ph:* Tony Gaudio. *Art. dir:* John J. Hughes. *Ed:* William Clemens. *Music:* Allie Wrubel and Mort Dixon; Sammy Fain and Irving Kahal; Bert Kalmar and Harry Ruby. *Songs:* "Massaging Window Panes"; "Beauty Must Be Loved"; "Pop Goes Your Heart"; "All on Account of a Strawberry Sundae." *Cost:* Orry-Kelly. *With* Dick Powell (*Bob Lane*), Josephine Hutchinson (*Joan Bradford*), John Halliday (*Henry Bradford*), Frank McHugh (*Tom Bradley*), Allen Jenkins (*Chuck*), Dorothy Dare, Ruth Donnelly, Marjorie Gateson, Russell Hicks, Mary Treen, J. M. Kerrigan, Mary Russell, Gavin Gordon, Mary Forbes, Jane Darwell. *Assoc. prod:* Sam Bischoff for Warner Brothers. 86m.

OIL FOR THE LAMPS OF CHINA (1935). Pat O'Brien's zealous loyalty to his company in an overseas posting in China creates a number of personal crises and moral dilemmas in his married life. *Sc:* Laird Doyle (a novel by Alice Tisdale Hobart). *Ph:* Tony Gaudio. *Art dir:* Robert Haas. *Ed:* William Clemens.

Music dir: Leo Forbstein. *With* Pat O'Brien (*Stephen Chase*), Josephine Hutchinson (*Hester*), Jean Muir (*Alice*), Lyle Talbot (*Jim*), John Eldredge (*Don*), Arthur Byron, Henry O'Neill, Donald Crisp, Ronnie Cosby, Willie Fung, Tetsu Komai, George Meeker, Christian Rub, Edward McWade, Florence Fair, William Davidson, Joseph Crehan, Keye Luke, Willard Robertson. *Prod:* Robert Lord for Cosmopolitan/First National. 110m.

PAGE MISS GLORY (1935). Comic send-up of beauty contests in which a chambermaid is elected as America's Sweetheart by a freak circumstance, and creates numerous problems for the promoters when she falls in love with the nation's top aviator. *Sc:* Delmer Daves, Robert Lord (a play by Joseph Schrank, Philip Dunning). *Ph:* George Folsey. *Art dir:* Robert Haas. *Ed:* William Clemens. *Music:* Harry Warren, Al Dubin. *Cost:* Orry-Kelly. *With* Marion Davies (*Loretta*), Pat O'Brien (*Click Wiley*), Dick Powell (*Bingo Nelson*), Mary Astor (*Gladys*), Frank McHugh (*Ed Olsen*), Lyle Talbot, Patsy Kelly, Allen Jenkins, Barton MacLane, Hobart Cavanaugh, Joseph Cawthorn, Al Shean, Berton Churchill, Helen Lowell, Mary Treen, Harry Beresford, Gavin Gordon, Lionel Stander, Joseph Crehan. *Prod:* Robert Lord for Cosmopolitan/Warner Brothers. 90m.

I FOUND STELLA PARISH (1935). To keep the facts of her past from her child, a famous English stage star flees to America, but is betrayed by an English newsman she loves; she sends the child away, and sinks to appearances in 'true confession' burlesque shows . . . but all ends well. *Sc:* Casey Robinson (a story

Mervyn LeRoy, Jack L. Warner, and (right) Hal B. Wallis pose with Marion Davies during PAGE MISS GLORY

by John Monk Saunders). *Ph:* Sid Hickox. *Art dir:* Robert Haas. *Ed:* Ralph Dawson, William Clemens. *Music dir:* Leo Forbstein. *With* Kay Francis (*Stella Parish*), Ian Hunter (*Keith Lockridge*), Paul Lukas (*Stephen Norman*), Sybil Jason (*Gloria Parish*), Jessie Ralph (*Nana*), Barton MacLane, Eddie Acuff, Joseph Sawyer, Walter Kingsford, Harry Beresford, Robert Strange. *Prod:* Harry Joe Brown for First National. 84m.

SWEET ADELINE (1935). A peculiar blending of spies, comedy and operetta in this adaptation of a Kern & Hammerstein stage success. *Sc:* Edwin S. Gelsey (a play by Jerome Kern, Oscar Hammerstein II). *Ph:* Sol Polito. *Art dir:* Robert Haas. *Ed:* Harold McLernon. *Music:* Jerome Kern, Oscar Hammerstein II. *Songs:* "Here Am I"; "Don't Ever Leave Me"; "Why Was I Born?"; " 'Twas Not So Long Ago"; "We Were So Very Young." *Cost:* Orry-Kelly. *Ensemble dir:* Bobby Connolly. *With* Irene Dunne (*Adeline*), Donald Woods (*Sid Barnett*), Hugh Herbert (*Rupert Rockingham*), Ned Sparks (*Dan Herzig*), Joseph Cawthorn (*Oscar Schmidt*), Louis Calhern, Winifred Shaw, Nydia Westman, Dorothy Dare, Phil Regan, Don Alvarado, Jack Mulhall, Noah Beery. *Prod:* Edward Chodorov for Warner Brothers. 87m.

ANTHONY ADVERSE (1936). Taken from a mammoth novel, the film follows the bastard hero's progress to manhood, his romance with a childhood sweetheart, travels in Africa and Cuba, and battles with an unscrupulous Spanish Grandee, culminating in his departure for America with his son. *Sc:* Sheridan Gibney (a novel by Hervey Allen). *Ph:* Tony Gaudio. *Art dir:* Anton Grot. *Ed:* Ralph Dawson. *Music:* Erich Wolfgang Korngold. *With* Fredric March (*Anthony Adverse*), Edmund Gwenn (*John Bonnyfeather*), Claude Rains (*Don Luis*), Olivia de Havilland (*Angela Guessippi*), Anita Louise (*Maria*), Louis Hayward (*Denis Moore*), Gale Sondergaard, Steffi Duna, Billy Mauch, Akim Tamiroff, Donald Woods, Ralph Morgan, Henry O'Neill, Pedro de Cordoba, George E. Stone, Luis Alberni, Fritz Leiber, Joseph Crehan, Rafaela Ottiano, Rollo Lloyd, Leonard Mudie, Scotty Beckett, Paul Sotoff, Frank Reicher, Clara Blandick, Marilyn Knowlden, Mathilde Comont, Eily Malyon, J. Carroll Naish, Addison Richards, William Riccardi, Grace Stafford, Boris Nicholai. *Prod:* Jack L. Warner and Henry Blanke for Warner Brothers. 140m.

THREE MEN ON A HORSE (1936). Madcap comedy about a tippling poet with a preternatural skill in picking winning racehorses who is kidnapped by a trio of bettors while his frantic boss tries to get him back in time to compose rhymes for Mother's Day cards! *Sc:* Laird Doyle (a play by John Cecil Holm, George Abbott). *Ph:* Sol Polito. *Art dir:* Robert Haas. *Ed:* Ralph Dawson. *Music dir:* Leo Forbstein. *With* Frank McHugh (*Erwin Trowbridge*), Joan Blondell (*Mabel*), Guy Kibbee (*Carver*), Carol Hughes (*Audrey Trowbridge*), Allen Jenkins (*Charlie*), Sam Levene, Teddy Hart, Edgar Kennedy, Paul Harvey, Margaret Irving, George Chandler, Harry Davenport, Tola Nesmith, Eily Malyon. *Assoc. prod:* Sam Bischoff for First National. 88m.

THE KING AND THE CHORUS GIRL (1937). Good production values enhance this self-explanatory comedy with Belgian Fernand Gravet whom Warners were trying to launch to international stardom. *Sc:* Norman Krasna, Groucho Marx. *Ph:* Tony Gaudio. *Art dir:* Robert Haas. *Ed:* Thomas Richards. *Music:* Werner Richard Heymann, Ted Koehler, *Dance dir:* Bobby Connolly. *Cost:* Orry-Kelly. *With* Fernand Gravet (*King Alfred*), Joan Blondell (*Dorothy*), Edward Everett Horton (*Count Humbert*), Alan Mowbray (*Donald*), Jane Wyman (*Babette*), Mary Nash, Luis Alberni, Kenny Baker, Shaw & Lee, Lionel Pape, Leonard Mudie, Adrian Roseley. *Prod:* Mervyn LeRoy for Warner Bros. 94m.

THEY WON'T FORGET (1937). Le-Roy's last good film at Warners: a swinging indictment of mob rule and lynch law, that catapulted Lana Turner to fame. *Sc:* Robert Rossen, Aben Kandel (novel "Death in the Deep South" by Ward Greene). *Ph:* Arthur Edeson. *Art dir:* Robert Haas. *Ed:* Thomas Richards. *Music:* Adolf Deutsch. *With* Claude Rains (*Andy Griffin*), Gloria Dickson (*Sybil Hale*), Edward Norris (*Robert Hale*), Otto Kruger (*Michael Gleason*), Lana Turner (*Mary Clay*), Allyn Joslyn, Linda Perry, Elisha Cook Jr., Cy Kendall, Clinton Rosemond, E. Alyn Warren, Elizabeth Risdon, Clifford Soubier, Granville Bates, Anne Shoemaker, Paul Everton, Donald Briggs, Sybil Harris, Trevor Bardette, Elliott Sullivan, Wilmer Hines, Eddie Acuff, Frank Faylen, Leonard Mudie, Harry Beresford, Edward Mc-Wade, John Ridgely. *Prod:* Mervyn Le-Roy for First National. 96m.

LeRoy produced THE GREAT GARRICK (1937, James Whale).

FOOLS FOR SCANDAL (1938). Off-beat comedy about an impoverished young nobleman being hired as a butler by a movie actress with whom he falls in love: a surprise climax presents the action as part of a stage play. *Sc:* Herbert & Joseph Fields (play "Return Engagement" by Nancy Hamilton, James Shute, Rosemary Casey). *Add. dial:* Irving Brecher. *Ph:* Ted Tetzlaff. *Art dir:* Anton Grot. *Ed:* William Holmes. *Music and lyrics:* Richard Rodgers, Lorenz Hart. *Music arranger:* Adolph Deutsch. "La Petite Harlem" *sequence dir. by:* Bobby Connolly. *With* Carole Lombard (*Kay Winter*), Fernand Gravet (*Rene*), Ralph Bellamy (*Philip Chester*), Allen Jenkins

(*Dewey Gibson*), Isabel Jeans (*Lady Paula Malveston*), Marie Wilson, Marcia Ralston, Tola Nesmith, Heather Thatcher, Jacques Lory, Tempe Piggott, Michellette Burani, Jeni LeGon. *Prod:* Mervyn LeRoy for Warner Brothers. 81m.

With the completion of FOOLS FOR SCANDAL, LeRoy left to join M-G-M. as a producer.

Films solely as producer:

STAND UP AND FIGHT (1938, W. S. Van Dyke).

DRAMATIC SCHOOL (1938, Robert B. Sinclair).

AT THE CIRCUS (1938, Edward Buzzell.

THE WIZARD OF OZ (1939, Victor Fleming).

Director:

WATERLOO BRIDGE (1940). Oft-filmed tale of a tragic romance between a ballet dancer and an officer from a rich background during the First World War. *Sc:* S. N. Behrman, George Froeschel, Hans Rambeau (a play by Robert E. Sherwood). *Ph:* Joseph Ruttenberg. *Art dir:* Cedric Gibbons. *Ed:* George Boemler. *Music:* Herbert Stothart. *Ballet staged by:* Ernst Matray. *With* Vivien Leigh (*Myra*), Robert Taylor (*Roy Cronin*), Lucile Watson (*Lady Margaret Cronin*), Virginia Field (*Kitty*), Maria Ouspenskaya (*Madame Olga Kirowa*), C. Aubrey Smith, Janet Shea, Janet Waldo, Steffi Duna, Virginia Carroll, Leda Nicova, Florence Baker, Margaret Manning, Frances MacInerney, Eleanor Stewart, Clara Reid, Leo G. Carroll, Jimmy Aubrey, Norma Varden, Wilfrid Lucas, Leonard Mudie, Gilbert Emery, Ethel Griffies, Phyllis Barry. *Prod:* Sidney Franklin for M-G-M. 102m. Other ver-

Vivien Leigh and Robert Taylor in WATERLOO BRIDGE

sions were *Waterloo Bridge* (1931, James Whale) and *Gaby* (1956, Curtis Bernhardt).

ESCAPE (1940). An anti-Nazi melodrama, re-teaming Taylor and Norma Shearer at the head of a largely European émigré cast. *Sc:* Arch Oboler, Marguerite Roberts (a novel by Ethel Vance). *Ph:* Robert Planck. *Art dir:* Cedric Gibbons, Urie McCleary. *Ed:* George Boemler. *Music:* Franz Waxman. *With* Norma Shearer (*Countess Von Treck*), Robert Taylor (*Mark Preysing*), Conrad Veidt (*General Kurt von Kolb*), Nazimova (*Emmy Ritter*), Felix Bressart (*Fritz Keller*), Albert Bassermann, Philip Dorn,

Bonita Granville, Edgar Barrier, Elsa Bassermann, Blanche Yurka, Lisa Golm. *Prod:* A Mervyn LeRoy Production for M-G-M. 104m. Re-issued as *When the Door Opened.*

BLOSSOMS IN THE DUST (1941). The true story of Edna Gladney, an American woman who overcame personal tragedy to fight for the recognition of the rights of illegitimate children; highly romanticised, but important as LeRoy's first colour film. *Sc:* Anita Loos (a story by Ralph Wainwright). *Ph:* Karl Freund, Howard Greene [Technicolor]. *Art dir:* Cedric Gibbons, Urie McCleary. *Ed:* George Boemler. *Music:* Herbert Stoth-

LeRoy menaces Joe Downing between scenes of UNHOLY PARTNERS watched by Edward G. Robinson

art. *With* Greer Garson (*Edna Gladney*), Walter Pidgeon (*Sam Gladney*), Felix Bressart (*Dr. Max Breslar*), Marsha Hunt (*Charlotte*), Fay Holden (*Mrs. Kahly*), Samuel S. Hinds, Kathleen Howard, George Lessey, William Henry, Henry O'Neill, John Eldridge, Clinton Rosemond, Theresa Harris, Charles Arnt, Cecil Cunningham, Ann Morris, Richard Nichols, Pat Barker, Mary Taylor, Marc Lawrence. *Prod:* Irving Asher for M-G-M. A Mervyn LeRoy Production. 99m.

UNHOLY PARTNERS (1941). LeRoy borrowed Edward G. Robinson from Warner Brothers to star in this comedy-drama about the criminal fraternity. *Sc:* Earl Baldwin, Bartlett Cormack, Lesser Samuels. *Ph:* George Barnes. *Art dir:* Cedric Gibbons, Urie McCleary(?). *Ed:* Harold F. Kress. *Music:* David Snell. *With* Edward G. Robinson (*Bruce Corey*), Edward Arnold (*Merrill Lambert*), Laraine Day (*Miss Cronin*), Marsha Hunt (*Gail Fenton*), William T. Orr (*Tommy Jarvis*), Don Beddoe, Walter Kingsford, Charles Cane, Charles Dingle, Charles Halton, Joseph Downing, Clyde Fillmore, Emory Parnell, Don Costello, Marcel Dalio, Frank Faylen, William Benedict, Charles B. Smith, Frank Dawson, Tom Seidel, Tom O'Rourke, George Ovey, Al Hill, Jay Novello, John Lilson, Billy Mann, Ann Morrison, Lester Scharff, June MacCloy, Larraine Kreuger, Natalie Thompson, Florine McKinney, Charles Jordan, Ann Pennington, Lee Phelps, Lester Dorr, Gertrude Bennett, Estelle Etterre, Milton Kibbee. *Prod:* Sam Marx for M-G-M. 94ms.

JOHNNY EAGER (1941). Melodramatic gangster yarn about a suave gangster whose fate is sealed when he falls for a beautiful, honest girl. *Sc:* John Lee Mahin, James Edward Grant (a story by James Edward Grant). *Ph:* Harold Rosson. *Art dir:* Cedric Gibbons, Stan Rogers. *Ed:* Albert Akst. *Music:* Bronislau Kaper. *With* Robert Taylor (*Johnny Eager*), Lana Turner (*Lisbeth Bond*), Edward Arnold (*John Benson Parnell*), Van Heflin (*Jeff Hartnett*), Robert Sterling (*Jimmy Courtney*), Patricia Dane, Glenda Farrell, Henry O'Neill, Diana Lewis, Barry Nelson, Charles Dingle, Paul Stewart, Cy Kendall, Don Costello, Lou Lubin, Joseph Downing, Connie Gilchrist, Robin Raymond, Leona Maricle, Byron Shores. *Prod:* John W. Considine Jr. for M-G-M. 107m.

RANDOM HARVEST (1942). Tearjerker about the love between an amnesiac soldier and an impulsive Scottish lass, enhanced by good acting and superior production values. *Sc:* Claudine West, George Froeschel, Arthur Wimperis (a novel by James Hilton). *Ph:* Joseph Ruttenberg. *Art dir:* Cedric Gibbons, Randall Duell. *Ed:* Harold F. Kress. *Music:* Herbert Stothart. *Song:* "She's Ma Daisy" staged by Ernst Matray. *Gowns:* Kalloch. *With* Greer Garson (*Paula*), Ronald Colman (*Charles Rainier*), Philip Dorn (*Dr. Jonathan Benet*), Susan Peters (*Kitty*), Henry Travers (*Dr. Sims*), Reginald Owen, Bramwell Fletcher, Rhys Williams, Una O'Connor, Charles Waldron, Elizabeth Risdon, Melville Cooper, Margaret Wycherly, Norma Varden, Marta Linden, Ann Richards, Aubrey Mather, Jill Esmond, Arthur Margetson, Alan Napier, David Cavendish, Ivan Simpson, Marie de Becker, Harry Shannon. *Prod:* Sidney Franklin for M-G-M. 124m.

MADAME CURIE (1944). Another lavish and lengthy biography about the discoverer of penicillin. *Sc:* Paul Osborn, Paul H. Rameau (a novel by Eve Curie). *Ph:* Joseph Ruttenberg. *Art dir:* Cedric Gibbons. *Ed:* Harold F. Kress. *Music:* Herbert Stothart. *With* Greer Garson (*Madame Curie*), Walter Pidgeon (*Pierre Curie*), Henry Travers (*Eugene Curie*), Albert Bassermann (*Professor Jean Perot*), Robert Walker (*David LeGros*), C. Aubrey Smith, Dame May Whitty, Victor Francen, Elsa Bassermann, Reginald Owen, Van Johnson, Margaret O'Brien. *Prod:* Sidney Franklin for M-G-M. 124m.

THIRTY SECONDS OVER TOKYO (1945). The story of the man who led the first bombing raid on Tokyo in the Second World War. *Sc:* Dalton Trumbo (a book by Captain Ted W. Lawson, Robert Considine). *Ph:* Harold Rosson, Robert Surtees. *Art dir:* Cedric Gibbons, Paul Groesse. *Ed:* Frank Sullivan. *Music:* Herbert Stothart. *With* Van Johnson (*Lieutenant Ted Lawson*), Robert Walker (*David Thatcher*), Spencer Tracy (*Lieutenant-Colonel James H. Dolittle*), Phyllis Thaxter (*Ellen Lawson*), Tim Murdock (*Dean Davenport*), Scott McKay, Gordon McDonald, Don DeFore, Robert Mitchum, John R. Reilly, Horace [later Stephen] McNally, Louis Jean Heydt, Donald Curtis, William 'Bill' Phillips, Douglas Cowan, Paul Langton, Leon Ames, Bill Williams, Robert Bice, Benson Fong, Ching Wah Lee, Alan Napier, Ann Shoemaker, Dorothy Ruth Morris, Jacqueline White, Selena Royle, Moroni Olsen. *Prod:* Sam Zimbalist for M-G-M. 138m.

LeRoy produced an Academy Award winning documentary short called THE HOUSE I LIVE IN (1945) in collaboration with Frank Ross. It was directed by Axel Stordahl.

WITHOUT RESERVATIONS (1946). An uncharacteristic romantic comedy vehicle for John Wayne. *Sc:* Andrew Solt (a novel by Jane Allen, Mae Livingston). *Ph:* Milton H. Krasner. *Art dir:* Albert D'Agostino, Ralph Berger. *Ed:* Jack Ruggiero. *Music:* Roy Webb. *With* Claudette Colbert (*Kit*), John Wayne (*Rusty*), Don DeFore (*Dink*), Anne Triola (*Connie*), Phil Brown (*Soldier*), Frank Puglia, Thurston Hall, Dona Drake, Charles Arnt, Louella Parsons, Fernando Alvarado, Cary Grant [uncredited 'guest']. *Prod:* Jesse L. Lasky for RKO. 107m.

HOMECOMING (1948). Powerful star vehicle with rich, married doctor falling in love with his nurse during combat in the Second World War. *Sc:* Paul Osborn (adapted by Jan Lustig from a novel by Sidney Kingsley). *Ph:* Harold Rosson. *Art dir:* Cedric Gibbons, Randall Duell. *Ed:* John Dunning. *Music:* Bronislau Kaper. *With* Clark Gable (*Ulysses Delby Johnson*), Lana Turner (*Lieutenant Jane 'Snapshot' McCall*), Anne Baxter (*Penny Johnson*), John Hodiak (*Dr. Robert Sunday*), Ray Collins (*Lieutenant-Colonel Avery Silver*), Gladys Cooper, Cameron Mitchell, Marshall Thompson, Lurene Tuttle, Jessie Grayson, J. Louis Johnson, Eloise Hardt. *Prod:* Sidney Franklin in association with Gottfried Reinhardt for M-G-M. 113m.

LITTLE WOMEN (1949). Colour screen re-make of the famous novel. *Sc:* Andrew Solt, Sarah Y. Mason, Victor Heerman (a novel by Louisa May Alcott). *Ph:* Robert Planck, Charles Schoenbaum [Technicolor]. *Art dir:* Cedric Gibbons, Paul Groesse. *Ed:* Ralph E. Winters. *Music:* Adolph Deutsch. *With* June Allyson (*Jo*), Peter Lawford (*Laurie*), Margaret O'Brien (*Beth*), Elizabeth Taylor (*Amy*), Janet Leigh (*Meg*), Rossano Brazzi, Mary Astor, Lucile Watson, C. Aubrey Smith, Elizabeth Patterson, Leon Ames, Harry Davenport, Richard Stapley, Connie Gilchrist, Ellen Corby. *Prod:* Mervyn LeRoy for M-G-M. 121m. Previous version, in 1933, directed by George Cukor.

ANY NUMBER CAN PLAY (1949). Story of a big time gambler, both on the tables and in love. *Sc:* Richard Brooks (a novel by Edward Harris Heth). *Ph:* Harold Rosson. *Art dir:* Cedric Gibbons, Urie McCleary. *Ed:* Ralph E. Winters. *Music:* Lennie Hayton. *With* Clark Gable (*Charles Enley Kyng*), Alexis Smith (*Lou Kyng*), Wendell Corey (*Robbin Elcott*), Audrey Totter (*Alice Elcott*), Frank Morgan (*Jim Kurstyn*), Mary Astor, Lewis Stone, Barry Sullivan, Marjorie Rambeau, Edgar Buchanan, Leon Ames, Mickey Knox, Richard Rober, William Conrad, Darryl Hickman, Caleb Peterson, Dorothy Comingore, Art Baker. *Prod:* Arthur Freed for M-G-M. 112m.

EAST SIDE, WEST SIDE (1950). The title refers to the differing sides of the tracks from which the characters come in this dramatic social melodrama. *Sc:* Isobel Lennart (a novel by Marcia Davenport). *Ph:* Charles Rosher. *Art dir:* Cedric Gibbons, Randall Duell. *Ed:* Harold F. Kress. *Music:* Miklos Rozsa. *With* Barbara Stanwyck (*Jessie Bourne*), James Mason (*Brandon Bourne*), Van Heflin (*Mark Dwyer*), Ava Gardner (*Isabel Lorrison*), Cyd Charisse (*Rosa Senta*), Nancy Davis, Gale Sondergaard, William Conrad, Raymond Greenleaf, Douglas Kennedy, Bev-

Robert Taylor drops by for a chat with Mervyn LeRoy on the set of EAST SIDE WEST SIDE. The film's stars, Barbara Stanwyck and James Mason are seen conferring in the background

erley Michaels, William Frawley, Lisa Golm, Tom Powers. *Prod:* Voldemar Vetluguin for M-G-M. 108m.

QUO VADIS? (1950). Long-cherished LeRoy project about a Roman centurion who became a Christian; filmed on location in Italy. *Sc:* John Lee Mahin, S. N. Behrman, Sonya Levien from a novel by Henryk Sienkiewicz. *Ph:* Robert Surtees [Technicolor]. *Associate ph:* William V. Skall. *Art dir:* William A. Horning, Cedric Gibbons, Edward Carfagno. *Ed:* Ralph E. Winters. *Music:* Miklos Rozsa. *With* Robert Taylor (*Marcus Vinicius*), Deborah Kerr (*Lygia*), Leo Genn (*Petronius*), Peter Ustinov (*Nero*), Finlay Currie (*Peter*), Patricia Laffan, Abraham Sofaer, Marina Berti, Buddy Baer, Felix Aylmer, Nora Swinburne, Ralph Truman, Norman Wooland, Peter Miles, Geoffrey Dunn, Nicholas Hannen, D. A. Clarke-Smith, Rosalie Crutchley, John Ruodock, Arthur Walge, Elspeth March, Strelsa Brown, Alfredo Varelli, Roberto Ottaviano, William Tubbs, Pietro Tordi, Sophia Loren [extra]. *Prod:* Sam Zimbalist for M-G-M. 168m. Rumour has it that Elizabeth Taylor may have appeared as an extra for a joke while visiting the set during filming. Also filmed in 1902 by Pathe; 1912 (Enrico Guazzoni) in Italy; 1913 in Italy (3 reels only); 1923

(G. D'Annunzio, Georg Jacoby).

LOVELY TO LOOK AT (1952). Glossy re-make of the Rogers/Astaire musical, *Roberta*. *Sc:* George Wells, Harry Robin (additional dialogue by Andrew Solt) (the musical comedy, "Roberta," adapted from the novel by Alice Duer Miller). *Ph:* George Folsey [Technicolor]. *Art dir:* Cedric Gibbons, Gabriel Scognamillo. *Ed:* John McSweeney Jr. *Music:* Otto A. Harbach [original book and lyrics], Jerome Kern with additional and revised lyrics by Dorothy Field. *Music dir:* Carmen Dragon, Saul Chaplin. *Cost:* Adrian. Songs include: "Smoke Gets in Your Eyes"; "Lovely to Look At"; "I Won't Dance." *With* Kathryn Grayson (*Stephanie*), Red Skelton (*Al Marsh*), Howard Keel (*Tony Naylor*), Marge Champion (*Clarisse*), Gower Champion (*Jerry Ralby*), Ann Miller, Zsa Zsa Gabor, Kurt Kasznar, Marcel Dalio, Diana Cassidy. *Prod:* Jack Cummings for M-G-M. 102m. Re-make of *Roberta* (1935, William A. Seiter).

MILLION DOLLAR MERMAID (GB: THE ONE PIECE BATHING SUIT) (1952). The story of Annette Kellerman; a romantic biography, with lavish aquatic numbers staged by Busby Berkeley. *Sc:* Everett Freeman. *Ph:* George Folsey [Technicolor]. *Art dir:* Cedric Gibbons, Jack Martin Smith. *Editor:* John McSweeney Jr. *Music dir:* Adolph Deutsch. "Fountain" and "Smoke" numbers staged by Busby Berkeley. *With* Esther Williams (*Annette Kellerman*), Walter Pidgeon (*Frederick Kellerman*), Victor Mature (*Jimmy Sullivan*), David Brian (*Alfred Harper*), Jesse White (*Doc Cronnol*), Donna Corcoran, Maria Tallchief, Howard Freeman, Charles Watts, Wilton

Graff, Frank Ferguson, James Bell, James Flavin, Willis Bouchey. *Prod:* Arthur Hornblow Jr. for M-G-M. 115m.

LATIN LOVERS (1953). Another romantic musical extravaganza. *Sc:* Isobel Lennart. *Ph:* Joseph Ruttenberg [Technicolor]. *Art dir:* Cedric Gibbons, Gabriel Scognamillo. *Ed:* John McSweeney Jr.

Producer Joe Pasternak talks to LeRoy during production of LATIN LOVERS watched by stars Lana Turner and Ricardo Montalban

Music: Nicholas Brodszky. *Lyrics:* Leo Robin. *With* Lana Turner (*Nora Taylor*), Ricardo Montalban (*Roberto Santos*), John Lund (*Paul Chevron*), Louis Calhern (*Grandfather Santos*), Jean Hagen (*Anne Kellwood*), Eduard Franz, Beulah Bondi, Joaquin Garay, Archer MacDonald, Dorothy Neumann, Robert Burton, Rita Moreno. *Prod:* Joe Pasternak for M-G-M. 104m.

ROSE MARIE (1954). LeRoy's farewell to M-G-M, a musical re-make of a popular Thirties success about a Mountie getting his man *and* the girl. *Sc:* Ronald Millar, George Froeschel (the operetta). *Ph:* Paul Vogel [Eastman Color; Cinemascope]. *Art dir:* Cedric Gibbons, Merrill Pye. *Ed:* Harold F. Kress. *Music:* Otto A. Harbach, Oscar Hammerstein [book and lyrics]; Rudolph Friml, Herbert Stothart. *Additional music and lyrics:* Rudolph Friml, George Stoll, Herbert Baker. *Musical numbers:* Busby Berkeley. *Songs:* "Rose Marie"; "Song of the Mounties"; "I'm a Mountie Who Never Got His Man"; "Free to be Free"; "Indian Love Call"; "I Have the Love"; "Mounties' Lullaby"; "The Right Place For a Girl." *With* Ann Blyth (*Rose Marie Lemaitre*), Howard Keel (*Mike Malone*), Fernando Lamas (*James Severn Duval*), Bert Lahr (*Barney McCorkle*), Marjorie Main (*Lady Jane Dunstock*), Joan Taylor, Ray Collins, Chief Yowlachie. *Prod:* Mervyn LeRoy for M-G-M. 104m. Re-make of 1936 film, directed by W. S. Van Dyke; also silent version in 1928, directed by Lucien Hubbard.

STRANGE LADY IN TOWN (1955). LeRoy's final film with Greer Garson, a Western dealing with family suspicions. *Sc:* Frank Butler. *Ph:* Harold Rosson [WarnerColor; Cinemascope]. *Art dir:* Gabriel Scognamillo. *Ed:* Folmar Blangsted. *Music:* Dimitri Tiomkin. *Title song:* Ned Washington; sung by Frankie Laine. *With* Greer Garson (*Julia Garth*), Dana Andrews (*Rork O'Brien*), Cameron Mitchell (*David Garth*), Lois Smith (*Spurs O'Brien*), Walter Hampden (*Father Gabriel*), Gonzales Gonzales. *Prod:* Mervyn LeRoy for Warner Brothers. 118m.

MISTER ROBERTS (1955). The story of life aboard a cargo ship in the Pacific during the Second World War; LeRoy took over direction when John Ford fell ill. *Directors:* John Ford, Mervyn LeRoy, Joshua Logan [uncredited]. *Sc:* Frank Nugent, Joshua Logan (a play by Joshua Logan, Thomas Heggen and a novel by Thomas Heggin). *Ph:* Winton C. Hoch [WarnerColor; Cinemascope]. *Art dir:* Art Loel. *Ed:* Jack Murray. *Music:* Franz Waxman. *With* Henry Fonda (*Lieutenant [jg] Roberts*), James Cagney (*Captain*), Jack Lemmon (*Ensign Frank Thurlowe Pulver*), William Powell (*Doc*), Ward Bond (*C.P.O. Dowdy*), Betsy Palmer, Phil Carey, Nick Adams, Harry Carey Jr., Ken Curtis, Frank Aletter, Fritz Ford, Buck Kartalian, William Henry, William Hudson, Stubby Kruger, Harry Tenbrook, Perry Lopez, Robert Roark, Pat Wayne, Tige Andrews, Jim Moloney, Denny Niles, Francis Conner, Shug Fisher, Danny Borzage, Jim Murphy, Kathleen O'Malley, Maura Murphy, Mimi Doyle, Jeanne Murray-Vanderbilt, Lonnie Pierce, Martin Milner, Gregory Walcott, James Flavin, Jack Pennick, Duke Kahanamoko. *Prod:* Leland Hayward for Orange Productions/ Warner Brothers. 123m.

THE BAD SEED (1956). Drama about a psychotic little girl who disposes of people that upset her. *Sc:* John Lee Mahin (the play by Maxwell Anderson and a novel by William March). *Ph:* Harold Rosson. *Art dir:* John Beckman. *Ed:* Warren Low. *Music:* Alex North. *With* Nancy Kelly (*Christine*), Patty McCormack (*Rhoda*), Henry Jones (*Le Roy*), Eileen Heckart (*Mrs. Daigle*), Evelyn Varden (*Monica*), William Hopper, Paul Fix, Jesse White, Gage Clarke, Joan Croyden, Frank Cady. *Prod:* Mervyn LeRoy for Warner Brothers. 129m.

TOWARD THE UNKNOWN (GB: BRINK OF HELL) (1956). Korean war flier who broke down under torture tries to re-establish himself as a test pilot. *Sc:* Beirne Lay Jr. *Phot:* Harold Rosson [WarnerColor; Warnerscope]. *Art dir:* John Beckman. *Ed:* William Ziegler. *Music:* Paul Baron. *Second Unit dir:* Russ Saunders. *Ph:* Harold E. Wellman. *Ed:* Thomas Reilly. *With* William Holden (*Major Lincoln Bond*), Lloyd Nolan (*Brigadier-General Banner*), Virginia Leith (*Connie Mitchell*), Charles McGraw (*Colonel Mickey McKee*), Murray Hamilton (*Major Bromo Lee*), L. Q. Jones, Karen Steele, Paul Fix, James Garner, Ralph Moddy, Maura Murphy. *Prod:* Mervyn LeRoy for Toluca Productions/Warner Brothers. 115m.

NO TIME FOR SERGEANTS (1958). Hillbilly becomes Army barrack-room joke; he and a pal fall out of a plane on their first flight, and are posted 'missing, believed dead', but then turn up for their lavish official funeral. *Sc:* John Lee Mahin (a play by Ira Levin and a novel by Mac Hyman). *Ph:* Harold Rosson. *Art dir:* Malcolm Brown. *Ed:* William Ziegler. *Music:* Ray Heindorf. *With* Andy Griffith (*Will Stockdale*), William Fawcett (*Pa Stockdale*), Murray Hamilton (*Irvin Blanchard*), Nick Adams (*Ben Whitledge*), Myron McCormick (*Sergeant King*), Bartlett Robinson, Jean Willes. *Prod:* Mervyn LeRoy for Warner Brothers. 110m.

HOME BEFORE DARK (1958). Fresh from a breakdown in a mental home, a college professor's wife returns to her husband, and nearly loses her sanity again until she overcomes her obsessional love for him, and puts her house in order. *Sc:* Eileen Bassing, Robert Bassing (a novel by Eileen Bassing). *Ph:* Joseph F. Biroc. *Art dir:* John Beckman. *Ed:* Philip W. Anderson. *Music dir:* Ray Heindorf. *Theme Song:* Jimmy McHugh, with lyrics by Sammy Cahn; sung by Mary Kaye. *With* Jean Simmons (*Charlotte Brown*), Dan O'Herlihy (*Arnold Brown*), Rhonda Fleming (*Joan Carlisle*), Efrem Zimbalist Jr. (*Jake Diamond*), Mabel Albertson (*Inez Winthrop*), Steve Dunne, Joan Weldon, Joanna Barnes, Kathryn Card. *Prod:* Mervyn LeRoy for Mervyn LeRoy Productions/Warner Brothers. 137m.

THE FBI STORY (1959). Panoramic saga, following the career of agent Chip Hardesty from enlistment to retirement against a mini-history of the law enforcement agency's various functions. *Sc:* Richard L. Breen, John Twist (a book by Don Whitehead). *Ph:* Joseph F. Biroc [WarnerColor; Warnerscope]. *Art dir:* John Beckman. *Ed:* Philip W. Anderson. *Music:* Max Steiner. *With* James Stewart (*Chip Hardesty*), Vera Miles (*Lucy*), Murray Hamilton (*Sam Crandall*), Larry Pennell (*George Crandall*), Nick Adams (*Jack Graham*), Diane Jergens, Jean Willes, Joan Taylor, Victor Millan, Parley

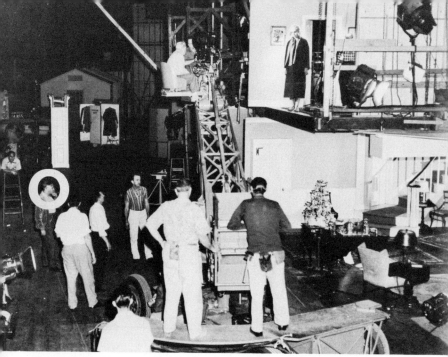

Mervyn LeRoy (head circled) directs HOME BEFORE DARK

Baer, Fay Roope, Ed Prentiss, Robert Gist, Buzz Martin, Kenneth Mayer, Paul Genge, Ann Doran, Forrest Taylor. *Prod:* Mervyn LeRoy for Mervyn LeRoy Productions/Warner Brothers. 149m.

WAKE ME WHEN IT'S OVER (1960). A restaurant proprietor, accidentally called for reserve duty, is posted to a remote Japanese island, where he enlists local aid and army war surplus material to build a luxury hotel. Business booms until the arrival of a Congressional Committee . . . *Sc:* Richard L. Breen (a novel by Howard Singer). *Ph:* Leon Shamroy [De Luxe Color; Cinemascope]. *Art dir:* Lyle R. Wheeler, John Beckman. *Ed:* Aaron Stell. *Music:* Cyril J. Mockridge. *Title Song:* Sammy Cahn, Jimmy Van Heusen; sung by Andy Williams. *With* Dick Shawn (*Gus Brubaker*), Ernie Kovacs (*Captain Stark*), Jack Warden (*Doc Farrington*), Margo Moore (*Lieutenant*

THE HOLLYWOOD PROFESSIONALS

LeRoy and James Stewart study
the script of THE FBI STORY

Nora McKay), Nobu McCarthy (*Ume*),
Don Knotts, Robert Strauss, Noreen Nash,
Robert Emhardt, Parley Baer, Raymond
Bailey, Frank Behrens, Linda Wong.
Prod: Mervyn LeRoy for Mervyn LeRoy
Productions/20th Century-Fox. 126m.

THE DEVIL AT 4 O'CLOCK (1961).
Convicts and a priest help evacuate a
leper hospital when an earthquake de-
stroys the island where the hospital is
situated. *Sc:* Liam O'Brien (a novel by
Max Catto). *Ph:* Joseph F. Biroc [East-
man Color]. *Art dir:* John Beckman. *Ed:*
Charles Nelson. *Music:* George Duning.
With Spencer Tracy (*Father Matthew
Doonan*), Frank Sinatra (*Harry*), Ker-
win Matthews (*Father Joseph Perreau*),
Jean Pierre Aumont (*Jacques*), Gregoire
Aslan (*Marcel*), Alexander Scourby, Barbara Luna, Cathy Lewis, Bernie Hamilton, Martin Brandt, Lou Merrill, Marcel

Dalio, Tom Middleton, Ann Duggan,
Louis Mercier, Michele Montau, Tony
Maxwell, Nanette Tanaka, Jean Del Val,
Moki Hana, Warren Hsieh, William
Keaulani, "Lucky" Luck, Norman Josef
Wright, Robin Shimatsu. *Prod:* Mervyn
LeRoy for Columbia. 126m.

A MAJORITY OF ONE (1961). Long-
winded romance between a Japanese
businessman and a Brooklyn Jewess. *Sc:*
Leonard Spigelgass (his play). *Ph:* Harry
Stradling Sr. [Technicolor]. *Art dir:* John
Beckman. *Ed:* Philip W. Anderson. *Music:*
Max Steiner. *Cost:* Orry-Kelly. *With* Rosa-
lind Russell (*Mrs. Jacoby*), Alec Guin-
ness (*Koichi Asano*), Ray Danton (*Jerome
Black*), Madlyn Rhue (*Alice Black*), Mae
Questel (*Mrs. Rubin*), Marc Marno,
Gary Vinson, Sharon Hugueny, Frank
Wilcox, Alan Mowbray, Francis De Sales,
Harriett MacGibbon. *Prod:* Mervyn Le-
Roy for Warner Brothers. 156m.

GYPSY (1962). Musical based on the
attempts of young Gypsy Rose Lee to
break away from the influence of her
domineering mother. *Sc:* Leonard Spigelgass (the stage musical). *Ph:* Harry Stradling Sr. [Technicolor; Technirama]. *Art
dir:* John Beckman. *Ed:* Philip W. Ander-
son. *Music:* Jule Styne; Arthur Laurents
[book]; Stephen Sondheim [lyrics].
Songs included: "Together"; "You're
Gonna Hear from Me"; "You Gotta Get
a Gimmick." *With* Rosalind Russell
(*Rose*), Natalie Wood (*Louise*), Karl
Malden (*Herbie Sommers*), Paul Wallace
(*Tulsa*), Betty Bruce (*Tessie Tura*),
Parley Baer, Harry Shannon, Suzanne
Cupito, Ann Jilliann, Diana Pace, Faith
Dane, Roxanne Arlen, Jean Willes,
George Petrie, James Milhollin, Ben
Lessy. *Prod:* Mervyn LeRoy for Warner

Brothers. 149m.

MARY, MARY (1963). A recently divorced couple find new partners but a meeting to sort out income tax problems eventually leads to them being reunited after a series of misunderstandings and petty jealousies. *Sc:* Richard L. Breen (a play by Jean Kerr). *Ph:* Harry Stradling Sr. [Technicolor]. *Art dir:* John Beckman. *Ed:* David Wages. *Music:* Frank Perkins. *With* Debbie Reynolds (*Mary*), Barry Nelson (*Bob*), Diane McBain (*Tiffany*), Hiram Sherman (*Oscar*), Michael Rennie (*Dirk*). *Prod:* Mervyn LeRoy for Warner Brothers. 125m.

MOMENT TO MOMENT (1965). A lonely housewife enters into an affair with a young naval officer, but it soon gets out of hand; thinking she has killed him during a struggle, she persuades a neighbor to help dispose of the body. But he is still alive, and as an amnesiac becomes a patient of the housewife's psychiatrist husband . . . *Sc:* John Lee Mahin, Alec Coppel (story "Laughs with a Stranger" by Alec Coppel). *Ph:* Harry Stradling, Sr. [Technicolor]. *Art dir:* Alexander Golitzen, Al Sweeney. *Ed:* Philip W. Anderson. *Music:* Henry Mancini. *Title song:* Henry Mancini, Johnny Mercer. *With* Jean Seberg (*Kay Stanton*), Honor Blackman (*Daphne Fields*), Sean Garrison (*Mark Dominic*), Arthur Hill (*Neil Stanton*), Peter Robbins (*Timmy*), Gregoire Aslan, Lomax Study, Donald Woods, Walter Reed, Albert Carrier, Richard Angarola, Georgette Anys. *Prod:* Mervyn LeRoy for Universal. 108m.

Mervyn LeRoy gives instructions to Natalie Wood on GYPSY

Index

Numbers in italics refer to illustrations